Dorothy L. Sayers:
Spiritual Writings

Cowley Publications is a ministry of the Society of St. John the Evangelist, a religious community for men in the Episcopal Church. Emerging from the Society's tradition of prayer, theological reflection, and diversity of mission, the press is centered in the rich heritage of the Anglican Communion.

Cowley Publications seeks to provide books, audio cassettes, and other resources for the ongoing theological exploration and spiritual development of the Episcopal Church and others in the body of Christ. To this end, it is dedicated to developing a new generation of theological writers, encouraging them to produce timely, creative, and stimulating publications of excellence, and making these publications available widely, reaching both clergy and lay persons.

Dorothy L. Sayers

SPIRITUAL WRITINGS

=

SELECTED AND INTRODUCED BY

ANN LOADES

COWLEY PUBLICATIONS
Cambridge • Boston
Massachusetts

Published in the United States of America by Cowley Publications, a
division of the Society of St. John the Evangelist. No portion of this book
may be reproduced, stored in or introduced into a retrieval system, or
transmitted, in any form or by any means—including photocopying—
without the prior written permission of Cowley Publications, except in the
case of brief quotations embodied in critical articles and reviews.

International Standard Book Number: 1–56101–066–9
Library of Congress Number: 93–15410

Library of Congress Cataloging-in-Publication Data

Sayers, Dorothy L. (Dorothy Leigh). 1893–1957.
Spiritual writings / Dorothy L. Sayers: selected and introduced
by Ann Loades.
p.   cm.
1. Theology.   2. Sayers, Dorothy L. (Dorothy Leigh), 1893–1957—
Religion.   I. Loades, Ann, 1950–   . II. Title.
BR85.S23   1993
230—dc20   93–15410

Cowley Publications
28 Temple Place
Boston, Massachusetts 02111

Printed in Great Britain at
the University Press, Cambridge

Contents

=

INTRODUCTION

=

Many of us have read Dorothy Leigh Sayers' detective fiction, but her spiritual writings are less familiar to us. It is rewarding and enjoyable because she writes it in so many different ways, as this book will show. Above all, we may come to some initial appreciation of her reading and translation of Dante's *Divine Comedy* on which she became something of an expert in the last fifteen years of her life. She translated and interpreted his work for the newly founded Penguin Classics series, and lectured on him to specialist and non-specialist audiences. When we come to look at her engagement with Dante's work, we will be able to see how he encouraged her to bring some neglected theological themes back into play, and so enlarged her own theological vision and imagination. She found in Dante a theologian comparable to Aquinas, but far more exciting. The poet was a man of 'passionate intellect', a phrase she used of herself after she had used it of him, for his formidable skills in exploring the 'good of the intellect' culminated in his ecstasy at the vision of God, and in his experience of his heart and will being moved by the love 'that moves the sun and the other stars'. We could not do justice to Dorothy Sayers unless we were able to take seriously her own conviction that 'Dante and I share the same faith'.

My own engagement with her work came about through the accident of reading *Unpopular Opinions* (1946), which included 'Are Women Human?' and 'The Human-not-quite-Human'. In the case of the former, an address given in 1938, she had talked about sex-equality with particular reference

1

to work, with women wanting as human beings much what men wanted, that is, 'interesting occupation, reasonable freedom for their pleasures, and a sufficient emotional outlet' (p. 114). The second essay (1941) linked her criticism to her concern for her religious tradition, and it is worth noting that it anticipates her reading of Dante, and the unmistakable evidence in his text that his evaluation of women differed in very important respects from that of Aquinas.

Women are not human. They lie when they say they have human needs: warm and decent clothing; comfort in the bus; interests directed immediately to God and His universe, not intermediately through any child of man. They are far above man to inspire him, far beneath him to corrupt him; they have feminine minds and feminine natures, but their mind is not one with their nature like the minds of men; they have no human mind and no human nature. . . .

God, of course, may have His own opinion, but the Church is reluctant to endorse it. . . .

Perhaps it is no wonder that the women were first at the Cradle and last at the Cross. They had never known a man like this Man — there never has been such another. A prophet and teacher who never nagged at them, never flattered or coaxed or patronised; who never made arch jokes about them, never treated them either as 'The women, God help us!' or 'The ladies, God bless them!'; who rebuked without querulousness and praised without condescension; who took their questions and arguments seriously; who never mapped out their sphere for them, never urged them to be feminine or jeered at them for being female; who had no axe to grind and no uneasy male dignity to defend; who took them as he found them and was completely unselfconscious. There is no act, no sermon, no parable in the whole Gospel that borrows its pungency from female perversity; nobody could possibly guess from the words and deeds of Jesus that there was anything 'funny' about woman's nature.

But we might easily deduce it from His contemporaries, and from His prophets before Him, and from His

Church to this day. Women are not human; nobody shall persuade that they are human; let them say what they like, we will not believe it, though One rose from the dead.

'The Human-not-quite-Human', UO pp. 121–2

Here then, in a collection of essays which serves as a lively introduction to her work as a journalist, essayist, lecturer and broadcaster, she was unambiguously writing as a theologian, and this set me off to read her non-detective-fiction. In the essay I have just quoted, as elsewhere in her work, she shows no interest in what might nowadays be called 'gender-inclusive' language for God, and she could rightly be described as in many ways a markedly conservative theologian, but she was at least determined to think about a humanly inclusive Christian anthropology. Both the essays I have mentioned are placed in the second section of *Unpopular Opinions* under the heading 'Political'. The first group of seven essays are headed 'Theological' and she tells us in her 'Foreword' that the first of these, on 'Christian Morality', was one of three so unpopular with the persons who commissioned them that they were suppressed before they appeared! Here, too, we may see why she is still well worth reading, for 'Christian morality' is an exercise on one of her favourite themes, denunciation of those who have capitulated to 'Caesar', that is, 'this present frame of mind in which it is assumed that the value of all work, and the value of all people, is to be assessed in terms of economics' (p. 11).

So far at least, there was enough to encourage me to suppose that there might well be more if I chose to look for it, but even so, nothing quite prepared me for the variety of literary forms in which her theology is explored. For instance, it was the word 'coinherence' which drew my attention to a poem called 'For Timothy, in the Coinherence' (p. 176), but nothing prepared me for the discovery that Timothy was a cat, and that he was being thought about in the light of lines from Dante's *Paradise*!

The immediate stimulus for this collection is twofold. 1993 is the centenary of her birth; and it is now half a century on from the first broadcasts of her twelve radio plays (begun

21 December 1941) published in 1943 as *The Man Born to be King*. These remain her best known work in the category of what I suppose we have to call 'religious drama' whether written for performance in cathedrals or on radio. After a few comments about her education and her life, I will introduce selections from her writing in more or less chronological order, so that the reader can follow her development as a theologian, culminating, as I have indicated above, in her discovery of Dante, and the contribution she made to enabling so many thousands of people in the immediate post-World War Two period to delight in his work in their turn. The connection between her own 'religious drama' and her reading of his is fundamentally a very simple one, I believe. Though a cat to his tiger as a poet, she like him wrote of 'the drama of the soul's choice', an important thread of connection in her work, not least in two of her pre-war Cathedral plays, *The Zeal of Thy House* (1937) and *The Devil to Pay* (1939). She found in Dante a poet able to mediate theology to his readers, and he made her a better theologian than she would otherwise have been.

1

EAST ANGLIA
AND OXFORD

=

Dorothy Sayers was the child of an East Anglian Church of
England parish to which her father had gone from Christ
Church Oxford. 'I recollect very well my first arrival at the
Rectory, wearing a brown pelisse and bonnet trimmed with
feathers, and accompanied by my nurse and my maiden aunt,
who carried a parrot in a cage' (Hone, p. 2).

> I was born in a hollow
> At a confluence of rivers.
> I was brought up in a swamp
> Carved, caged, counter-checked like a chessboard
> By dyke and drain,
> Running from the Great Ouse to the Wash
> Where the wind never stops blowing;
> I know all about the smell that comes off the drowned
> land
> When the waters turn home in the spring
> (A peculiar smell – and I have encountered something
> like it
> In Venice,
> In the *piccoli canali* in the moonlight,
> Where it is considered highly romantic);
> I can say to the gadabouts;
> 'If you must have dank smells, you can get them in the
> Fens of East Anglia . . .'

See 'Lord, I thank thee', p. 121

Her clerical father had the sense to teach her Latin from
when she was about seven, and by the age of thirteen her

French was almost as good as her English and her German not far short. Here were learned the elements of her skills as a translator, not only of the *Comedy* but of such works as *The Song of Roland*, the contribution to the Penguin Classics which so unfortunately interrupted the *Paradise* volume, left incomplete at her death. She had translated *Roland* once on completing her studies at Somerville, and returned to it so near to the end of her own life that it was published in 1957, the year of her own death.

Education at home was interrupted only by an illness-ridden period at school, and she won her way to Somerville in 1912, a college born of 'enlightened ideas, and in particular of a progressive conception of woman, which clothed itself in the hereditary feminine garb of modest manners and watchful tact' (Hone, p. 12).

From experience of East Anglian parishes as well as Oxford we may suppose was born her theological education (reared as she must have been on the tough intellectual diet of Prayer Book Matins and Evensong), as well as her capacity for utter boredom with intellectual and emotional anaemia in doctrine, especially in Christology. As she was to write: 'At the name of Jesus, every voice goes plummy, every gesture becomes pontifical, and a fearful creeping paralysis slows down the pace of the dialogue.' She had extensive experience of hearing the Bible read in churches, 'against the handicaps of an Elizabethan vocabulary, a solemn occasion, an over-powering background, a mute assembly, and acoustics with a two-second echo':

> Most unreal of all is the speech of the story's central character – every word a 'familiar quotation', pulpit-dissected, sifted, weighed, burdened with a heavy accretion of prophetic and exegetical importance. In a sense not contemplated by the Evangelist, we feel it to be true that never man spake as this man, for by this time the words have lost all likeness to the speech of a living person.

'Divine Comedy', UO p. 21

She was rightly perturbed by anything that smacked of unreality in any presentation of Christ: 'The Humanity is never really there – it is always just coming on, or just going off, or being a light or a shadow or a voice in the wings.' This sensitivity explains her written instructions to producers of her radio plays, and her insistence that one way of testing out a Christology was to put Christ at the centre of a dramatic production and try out the chracter there.

Her East Anglian background is obviously crucial to the writing of *The Nine Tailors* (1934), a book fortunate for us in that extracts from it enable us to include at least some material about Peter Wimsey in a book about Dorothy Sayers' theology! Readers of *Gaudy Night* (1935) may recall that Peter explains to Harriet that

> I have nothing much in the way of religion, or even morality, but I do recognise a code of behaviour of sorts. I do know that the worst sin – perhaps the only sin – passion can commit, is to be joyless. It must lie down with laughter or make its bed in hell – there is no middle way . . ..

GN ch XXIII, p. 478

Wimsey is not totally devoid of an aesthetic if not securely religious sensibility, however. In *The Nine Tailors* he is marooned in Fenchurch St Paul by the snow. He attends a late night service before taking his place among the change-ringers who with him are unwittingly to bring about a man's death, as though they were agents of an impersonal justice. His own experience of 'being entranced by wonder and delight' at the sight of the East Anglian pre-Reformation angel-roof is hers, as child and as adult (see p. 26). In her chapter on 'Pentecost' in *The Mind of the Maker* (1941) she cites the biblical and non-biblical poetry hovering in her memory when she wrote about those ranked angels (see pp. 70–2). And she has the temerity to put some of them literally on stage in *The Zeal of Thy House* among its cast – three Archangels, one Recording Angel, and a young cherub who is Thurifer to Raphael. James Brabazon's biography of her informs us that for the 1949 revival of *Zeal* it required eighty-eight yards of gold paper folded into half-inch pleats, then stuck with feathers, to furnish the Archangels in an appropriate magnificence (p. 250). They represent the glory of heaven, but it is not beyond Gabriel to pluck a feather from his own wing to be trimmed into a new pen for the Recording Angel. To make a thread of connection with Dante again, amongst many other things, the *Comedy* is about angelic presence, angelic aid to human freedom, as in the case of the one who comes to make sure that Dante and Virgil, his guide, can get into the City of Dis or Satan,

> Walking the water of Styx with unwet feet.
>
> His left hand, moving, fanned away the gross
> Air from his face, nor elsewise did he seem
> At all to find the way laborious.
>
> H 9.81–4

Dante was to make further sense, for Dorothy Sayers, of a vision of hierarchy, order and otherness in its inexhaustible variety, including that of 'super-human personality and differentiated power' as she was to call these beings, a realm which she (so to speak) inhabited without any sign of intellectual discomfort.

From the Fens and its angel-roofs, she went to Oxford and came under the formidable tutelage of Miss Mildred K. Pope, who published with Manchester University Press in 1934 a work entitled *From Latin to Modern French with Especial Consideration of Anglo-Norman*, the year in which she was appointed to a professorship there (Reynolds p. 6). In *Gaudy Night* we have Dorothy Sayers' lovingly but wryly observed portrait of a certain type of scholar. Miss Lydgate struggles to get through the press a book on the prosodic elements in English verse from Beowulf to Bridges, requiring twelve different varieties of type, five successive revises in galley form at different stages of completion, sheets in page proof, an appendix in typescript, and an introduction still to be written. Miss Lydgate had not and indeed could not capitulate to 'Caesar', nor would she score well in an equally insidious form of evaluation, that of 'performance indicators'. It is all too easy for us to forget what it was like for women to be in, but in a sense not of a university. If we re-read the description in *Gaudy Night* of the immense care with which Harriet puts on her academic dress, we can

8

perhaps recapture something of the feelings of those women who in October 1920 took their BA and MA degrees together. The experience of having been at Somerville in just that period must have been both extraordinary and invaluable. In any event, to the period of wartime and its aftermath belong some of Dorothy Sayers' first poems on religious themes — on death, penitence, the hope of redemption, and the hope of Paradise — all themes that will recur in her work.

Hymn in Contemplation of Sudden Death

Lord, if this night my journey end,
I thank Thee first for many a friend,
The sturdy and unquestioned piers
That run beneath my bridge of years.

And next, for all the love I gave
To things and men this side the grave,
Wisely or not, since I can prove
There always is much good in love.

Next, for the power thou gavest me
To view the whole world mirthfully,
For laughter, paraclete of pain,
Like April suns across the rain.

Also that, being not too wise
To do things foolish in men's eyes,
I gained experience by this,
And saw life somewhat as it is.

Next, for the joy of labour done
And burdens shouldered in the sun;
Nor less, for shame of labour lost,
And meekness born of a barren boast.

For every fair and useless thing
That bids men pause from labouring
To look and find the larkspur blue
And marigolds of a different hue;

For eyes to see and ears to hear,
For tongue to speak and thews to bear,
For hands to handle, feet to go,
For life, I give Thee thanks also.

For all things merry, quaint and strange,
For sound and silence, strength, and change,
And last, for death, which only gives
Value to every thing that lives;

For these, good Lord that madest me,
I praise Thy name; since, verily,
I of my joy have had no dearth,
Though this night were my last on earth.

Op. I (1916)

The Gates of Paradise

From the grave-bed and the winding sheet
Is a long way for dead feet,
A dark road for dead eyes,
That leads to the gates of Paradise.

When Judas' soul went through the night,
To knock on Hades gate,
His way was over the whin-pricked moor,
And the noise of the wind was great.

He had no lantern to his feet,
Nor candle in his hand,
Such as God gives to every man
That dies at the time planned.

The angels sit in highest Heaven
And trim the lamps of God,
And all day long make lights for those
That travel death's dim road.

And when the cross is on thy breast,
The chrism on thine eyes,
Thy angel will bear down thy light
Out of the starry skies
And thou therewith shalt walk by night
Safely to Paradise.

But whoso doth so deadly sin
To cast his life away,
Finding his lamp not lit betimes
Walks through the midnight grey.

For a long night and half a day
Did Judas walk alone
Through the utter dark, for in that place
Is neither sun nor moon.

For a long night and half a day
Did Judas vainly seek
To reach the gates of Paradise,
The salt tears on his cheek.

With that he saw a candle gleam
   Borne by a hasty man,
And Judas caught him by the cloak
   So swiftly as he ran.

'O let me walk with thee, kind friend –
   I grope, I fail, I fall,
I have no lamp nor candle-light
   And the night is over all.'

'Full gladly, so thou make good speed,
   I run to keep the tryst,
That was given to me at the gates of Hell,
   By sweet King Jesus Christ.

'I am the thief whom God forgave,
   On Calvary's bitter tree,
For "To-night," He said, "thou shalt rest thine head
   In Paradise, with Me."'

'And I am the man that sinned such a sin
   As the world remembers not,
That sold for a price the Lord of Life –
   Judas Iscariot.'

'Now God forbid, thou damnèd wretch,
   That ever this should be,
That I should tryst with Jesus Christ,
   In the company of thee.'

The first robber went his way,
   And Judas walked alone,
Mirk, mirk was the black midnight,
   The heavy wind made moan.

Right so there came a second man
   Was walking by the road:
'O brother, let me share thy light
   As far as Hell's abode.'

'Now well I fear, my brother dear,
   Thou never wilt walk with me –
I am that thief which railed on Christ
   All on His bitter tree.

'I cast shame on King Jesus then,
    Wearing His painful crown,
And scorn upon His Royal Head,
    Whence the pale sweat dripped down.

'O rudd-red were the five blest wounds
    Where nails and spear went in,
A thousand, thousand years of Purgatory fire
    Never can cleanse my sin.'

'Why never, I ween,' said Judas then
    'Did two such sinners meet;
I sold King Christ to the bloody Jews,
    That pierced His Hands and Feet.'

'Art thou that man,' quoth the robber,
    'Most cursed under skies?
God do so to me if I go with thee
    To the gates of Paradise!'

The second robber went his way,
    And Judas walked alone,
Till he was aware of a grey man,
    That sat upon a stone,
And the lamp he had in his right hand
    Shone brighter than the moon.

'Come hither, come hither, thou darkling man,
    And bear me company,
This lamp I hold will give us light,
    Enough for thee and me.'

Judas walks with the grey-clad man,
    And fear is in his heart:
'Speak yet again, thou man in grey
    And tell me what thou art.'

'I bought a burden of deadly sin,
    And needs must pay the price,
I bear it hither in my hand
    To the gates of Paradise.'

14

'Sin cannot lie upon thy heart
  So heavy as on mine.'
'Nay, sinner, whosoe'er thou art,
  'Tis a heavier load than thine.'
He hath not askèd Judas' name,
  And Judas makes no sign.

'If sin is heavy on thy heart,
  And I must bear its weight,
It is fit that we should go together
  To tryst at Hades gate.'

Judas walked with the grey-clad man
  And feared to tell his name,
He clasped his hand in the barren land,
  Bright burned the lanthorn's flame,
Brotherliwise and hand in hand,
  To Paradise they came.

Satan looked out from Hades gate,
  His hand upon the key,
'Good souls, before I let you in,
  First tell me who ye be.'

'We be two men that died of late
  And come to keep Hell's tryst,
This is Judas Iscariot,
  And I am Jesus Christ.'

Op. I (1916)

15

2

ANGELS AND MINISTERS
OF GRACE

=

To make a living, Dorothy Sayers turned to writing detective fiction, beginning with *Whose Body?* (1923). Soon she had an additional reason for the pursuit of success, for a son was born to her on 3 January 1924. Later she married a man who had children by his first marriage. It may have been in part because his children did not live with him that Anthony could not come to live with the woman he supposed had adopted him, whom he eventually came to realize was his mother. She seems to have managed the upbringing of her son as well as she possibly could in the circumstances, supporting him, and visiting him as he grew up in the household of a friend whom she trusted, but this may well have been at great personal and emotional cost to her as well as to her child. In her radio play *He That Should Come*, first broadcast on Christmas Day, 1938, the Nativity story, focusing on Mary, a mother with a newborn son, enables women, placed as was Dorothy Sayers, to express their tenderness for their children, no matter what the circumstances of their conception.

In *He That Should Come*, the 'three kings' of post-biblical tradition merely enact the Prologue and Epilogue; the Epiphany of the Child is central in a later play, first of the series of twelve called *The Man Born to be King*. An extract from the latter will be given in a later sequence. Here the selection begins with material from *He That Should Come*, with its echoes of her earlier poetic style. These are followed by readings from *The Nine Tailors*, taking us, as it were, from Christmas to Easter, and her entirely serious portrait of St Richard of Chichester, whose Book of Common Prayer feast day falls on April 3 – just the sort of saint to be honoured by the Rector and Mrs Venables, one feels.

16

Note to Producers (of *He That Should Come*)

The whole effect and character of the play depend on its being played in an absolutely natural and realistic style. Any touch of the ecclesiastical intonation or of 'religious unction' will destroy its intention. The whole idea in writing it was to show the miracle that was to change the whole course of human life enacted in a world casual, inattentive, contemptuous, absorbed in its own affairs and completely unaware of what was happening: to illustrate, in fact, the tremendous irony of history. It may be found advisable to make this point clear to the actors before they start, lest some preconceptions as to what is or is not 'reverent' in a Nativity Play should hamper the freedom of their performance. I feel sure that it is in the interests of a true reverence towards the Incarnate Godhead to show that His Manhood was a real manhood, subject to the common realities of daily life; that the men and women surrounding Him were living human beings, not just characters in a story; that, in short, He was born, not into 'the Bible', but into the world. . . . There will always be a few voices raised to protest against the introduction of 'reality' into religion; but I feel that the great obstacle in the path of Christianity today is that to so many it has become unreal, shadowy, 'a tale that is told', so that it is of the utmost importance to remind people by every means in our power that the thing actually happened – that it is, and was from the beginning, closely in contact with real life.

HTSC pp. 218–9

Adam and Eve stood under a tree,
  (*Four rivers in Paradise*)
A sweet and comely sight to see
For they were fair as fair could be,
Adam and Eve beneath the tree
  (*Paradise, Paradise*
  God is all in all).

And on the tree the branches grew
  (*Four rivers in Paradise*)
Adorned with leaves of tender hue,
And they were fair as fair could be
And Adam and Eve stood under the tree
  (*Paradise, Paradise,*
  God is all in all).

And on the branch a beauteous flower
  (*Four rivers in Paradise*)
Budded and bloomed from hour to hour,
The flower that on the branches grew
Adorned with leaves of tender hue,
And it was fair as fair could be
And Adam and Eve stood under the tree
  (*Paradise, Paradise,*
  God is all in all).

And in that flower a fruit of gold
  (*Four rivers in Paradise*)
Lay hid within the petals' fold,
The petals of the beauteous flower
That budded and bloomed from hour to hour,
The flower that on the branches grew
Adorned with leaves of tender hue,
And it was fair as fair could be
And Adam and Eve stood under the tree
  (*Paradise, Paradise,*
  God is all in all).

And bit that fruit unto the stone,
The strange, forbidden fruit of gold
That hid within the petals' fold,
The petals of the beauteous flower
That budded and bloomed from hour to hour,
The flower that on the branches grew
Adorned with leaves of tender hue,
And the tree withered down to the ground so bare,
And Adam and Eve stood naked there;
      (Paradise, Paradise,
      God is all in all).

But when the stone had fallen to earth,
      (Four rivers in Paradise)
It brought another tree to birth,
That tall and stately grew anon,
The tree that sprang from that fruit stone,
The strange forbidden fruit of gold
That hid within the petals' fold,
The petals of the beauteous flower
That budded and bloomed from hour to hour,
The flower that on the branches grew
Adorned with leaves of tender hue,
And it was fair as fair could be,
And Adam and Eve stood under the tree
      (Paradise, Paradise,
      God is all in all).

HTSC pp. 263–5

19

MARY (*sings*)
Balow-la-lee, my little king,
   What shall we do to comfort Thee?
Canst Thou for whom the angels sing
   Content Thee with balow-la-lee,
               Balow-la-lee?
Balow-la-lee, my royal child,
   There's little we can give to Thee,
A manger-bed, a mother mild,
   The ox and the ass for company,
               Balow-la-lee.

                        HTSC p. 271

BALTHAZAR

Out of the darkness, out of the desert,
Beyond the secret springs of the Nile
I have seen the fire of desire flare in the zenith
Scaring the crocodiles under the shadow of the pyramids.
The dusky gods have trembled, the witch-dancers are struck down
In the midst of their dances.
A cry is gone up in the halls of the dead, from the seven gates of
    the dead,
The cry of Isis over Osiris slain,
The birth-cry of Horus.
This is the end or else the beginning of all things,
And sorrow either way, between a cry and a cry;
Therefore I come, seeking the soul of sorrow,
Balthazar, King of Ethiopia, surnamed 'the Servant',
Following the Star.

HTSC Prologue pp. 224–5

BALTHAZAR

How much you need to content you!
The wisdom that sets the soul beyond the reach of suffering,
The power to abolish suffering. I am more humble;
I do not mind being ignorant and unhappy —
All I ask is the assurance that I am not alone,
Some courage, some comfort against this burden of fear and pain.
I am a servant, born of the seed of Ham,
The oppressed, the accurst;
My skin is black with the punishing fury of the sun.
About my palaces the jungle creeps and whines,
Famine and plague are my fireside companions,
And beyond the circle of the fire, the glare of hungry eyes.
The lion sits by the water-hole, where the women go down to
    wash,
In the branches crouches the leopard.
I look out between the strangling branches of the vine and see
Fear in the east, fear in the west; armies
And banners marching and garments rolled in blood.
Yet this is nothing, if only God will not be indifferent,
If He is beside me, bearing the weight of His own creation;
If I may hear His voice among the voices of the vanquished,
If I may feel His hand touch mine in the darkness,
If I may look upon the hidden face of God
And read in the eyes of God
That He is acquainted with grief.

HTSC Prologue p. 227

The Nine Tailors

The art of change-ringing is peculiar to the English, and, like most English peculiarities, unintelligible to the rest of the world. To the musical Belgian, for example, it appears that the proper thing to do with a carefully-tuned ring of bells is to play a tune upon it. By the English campanologist, the playing of tunes is considered to be a childish game, only fit for foreigners; the proper use of bells is to work out mathematical permutations and combinations. When he speaks of the music of his bells, he does not mean musicians' music – still less what the ordinary man calls music. To the ordinary man, in fact, the pealing of bells is a monotonous jangle and a nuisance, tolerable only when mitigated by remote distance and sentimental association. The change-ringer does, indeed, distinguish musical differences between one method of producing his permutations and another; he avers, for instance, that where the hinder bells run 7, 5, 6, or 5, 6, 7, or 5, 7, 6, the music is always prettier, and can detect and approve, where they occur, the consecutive fifths of Tittums and the cascading thirds of the Queen's change. But what he really means is, that by the English method of ringing the rope and wheel, each several bell gives forth her fullest and her noblest note. His passion – and it is a passion – finds its satisfaction in mathematical completeness and mechanical perfection, and as his bell weaves her way rhythmically up from lead to hinder place and down again, he is filled with the solemn intoxication that comes of intricate ritual faultlessly performed. To any disinterested spectator, peeping in upon the rehearsal, there might have been something a little absurd about the eight absorbed faces; the eight tense bodies poised in a spell-bound circle on the edges of eight dining-room chairs; the eight upraised right hands, decorously wagging the handbells upward and downward; but to the performers, everything was serious and important as an afternoon with the Australians at Lord's.

Mr Hezekiah Lavender having called three successive bobs, the bells came back into rounds without mishap.

NT pp. 25–6 'The First Course'

The eight men advanced to their stations, and Hezekiah consulted his watch.

'Time!' he said.

He spat upon his hands, grasped the sallie of Tailor Paul, and gently swung the great bell over the balance.

Toll-toll-toll; and a pause; toll-toll-toll; and a pause; toll-toll-toll; the nine tailors, or teller-strokes, that mark the passing of a man. The year is dead; toll him out with twelve strokes more, one for every passing month. Then silence. Then, from the faint, sweet tubular chimes of the clock overhead, the four quarters and the twelve strokes of midnight. The ringers grasped their ropes.

'Go!'

The bells gave tongue: Gaude, Sabaoth, John, Jericho, Jubilee, Dimity, Batty Thomas and Tailor Paul, rioting and exulting high up in the dark tower, wide mouths rising and falling, brazen tongues clamouring, huge wheels turning to the dance of the leaping ropes. Tin tan din dan bim bam bom bo – tan tin din dan bam bim bo bom – tin tan dan din bim bam bom bo – tan tin dan din bam bim bo bom – tan dan tin bam din bo bim bom – every bell in her place striking tuneably, hunting up, hunting down, dodging, snapping, laying her blows behind, making her thirds and fourths, working down to lead the dance again. Out over the flat, white wastes of fen, over the spear-straight, steel-dark dykes and the wind-bent, groaning poplar trees, bursting from the snow-choked louvres of the belfry, whirled away southward and westward in gusty blasts of clamour to the sleeping counties went the music of the bells – little Gaude, silver Sabaoth, strong John and Jericho, glad Jubilee, sweet Dimity and old Batty Thomas, with great Tailor Paul bawling and striding like a giant in the midst of them. Up and down went the shadows of the ringers upon the walls, up and down went the scarlet sallies flickering roofwards and floorwards, and up and down, hunting in their courses, went the bells of Fenchurch St Paul.

Wimsey, his eye upon the ropes and his ear pricked for the treble's shrill tongue speaking at lead, had little attention to give to anything but his task. He was dimly conscious of old Hezekiah, moving with the smooth rhythm of a machine, bowing his ancient back very slightly at each pull to bring Tailor Paul's great weight

24

over, and of Wally Pratt, his face anxiously contorted and his lips moving in the effort to keep his intricate course in mind. Wally's bell was moving down now towards his own, dodging Number Six and passing Number Five, striking her two blows at lead, working up again, while the treble came down to take her place and make her last snapping lead with Sabaoth. One blow in seconds place and one at lead, and Sabaoth, released from the monotony of the slow hunt, ran out merrily into her plain hunting course. High in the air above them the cock upon the weathervane stared out over the snow and watched the pinnacles of the tower swing to and fro with a slowly widening sweep as the tall stalk of stone gathered momentum and rocked like a wind-blown tree beneath his golden feet.

NT pp. 38–40 'The Second Course'

Wimsey made a hasty toilet and ran downstairs, Bunter following him decorously. They let themselves out by the front door, and, guided by Bunter's electric torch, made their way through the shrubbery and across the road to the church, entering just as the organ boomed out its final notes. Choir and parson were in their places and Wimsey, blinking in the yellow lamplight, at length discovered his seven fellow-ringers seated on a row of chairs beneath the tower. He picked his way cautiously over the cocoa-nut matting towards them, while Bunter, who had apparently acquired all the necessary information beforehand, made his unperturbed way to a pew in the north aisle and sat down beside Emily from the Rectory. Old Hezekiah Lavender greeted Wimsey with a welcoming chuckle and thrust a prayer-book under his nose as he knelt down to pray.

'Dearly beloved brethren — '

Wimsey scrambled to his feet and looked round.

At the first glance he felt himself sobered and awe-stricken by the noble proportions of the church, in whose vast spaces the congregation – though a good one for so small a parish in the dead of a winter's night – seemed almost lost. The wide nave and shadowy aisles, the lofty span of the chancel arch – crossed, though not obscured, by the delicate fan-tracery and crenellated moulding of the screen – the intimate and cloistered loveliness of the chancel, with its pointed arcading, graceful ribbed vault and five narrow east lancets, led his attention on and focused it first upon the remote glow of the sanctuary. Then his gaze, returning to the nave, followed the strong yet slender shafting that sprang fountain-like from floor to foliated column-head, spraying into the light, wide arches that carried the clerestory. And there, mounting to the steep pitch of the roof, his eyes were held entranced with wonder and delight. Incredibly aloof, flinging back the light in a dusky shimmer of bright hair and gilded outspread wings, soared the ranked angels, cherubim and seraphim, choir over choir, from corbel and hammer-beam floating face to face uplifted.

'My God!' muttered Wimsey, not without reverence. And he softly repeated to himself: 'He rode upon the cherubims and did fly; He came flying upon the wings of the wind.'

Mr Hezekiah Lavender poked his new colleague sharply in the

ribs, and Wimsey became aware that the congregation had settled down to the General Confession, leaving him alone and agape upon his feet. Hurriedly he turned the leaves of his prayer-book and applied himself to making the proper responses. Mr Lavender, who had obviously decided that he was either a half-wit or a heathen, assisted him by finding the Psalms for him and by bawling every verse very loudly in his ear.

'. . . Praise Him in the cymbals and dances: praise Him upon the strings and pipe.'

The shrill voices of the surpliced choir mounted to the roof, and seemed to find their echo in the golden mouths of the angels.

'Praise Him upon the well-tuned cymbals; praise Him upon the loud cymbals.

'Let everything that hath breath praise the Lord.'

NT pp. 35–6 'The Second Course'

The parish church of Fenchurch St Paul, like a good many others in that part of the country, stands completely isolated from the village itself, with only the Rectory to neighbour it. The village itself is grouped about a crossroads, one arm of which runs southward to Fenchurch St Stephen and northwards to join the Fenchurch St Peter road a little south of the Thirty-foot; while the other, branching off from the same road by the church, degenerates at the western end of the village into a muddy drove by which, if you are not particular about your footing, you may, if you like, emerge once more on to the road by the Thirty-foot at Frog's Bridge. The three Fenchurches thus form a triangle, with St Paul to the north, St Peter to the south, and St Stephen to the west. The L.N.E.R. line connects St Peter with St Stephen, passing north to cross the Thirty-foot at Dykesey Viaduct on its way to Leamholt.

... Fenchurch St Paul is the smallest village, and has neither river nor railway; it is, however, the oldest; its church is by far the largest and the noblest, and its bells beyond question the finest. This is due to the fact that St Paul is the original abbey foundation. The remains of the first Norman church and a few stones which mark the site of the old cloisters may still be seen to east and south of the existing chancel. The church itself, with the surrounding glebe, stands on a little mound rising some ten or twelve feet above the level of the village – an elevation which, for the Fens, is considerable and, in ancient times, was sufficient to save church and abbey from inundation during the winter months. As for the river Wale, Fenchurch St Peter has no right to boast about that, for did not the old course of the Wale run close by St Paul's church, until the cutting of Potter's Lode in King James I's time drained away its waters by providing them with a shorter and more direct channel? Standing on the roof of the tower at Fenchurch St Paul, you can still trace the old river bed, as it wanders circuitously across meadow and ploughland, and see where the straight green dyke of Potter's Lode spans it like a string to a bow. Outside the group of the Fenchurches, the land rises slightly all round, being drained by cross-dyking into the Wale.

NT pp. 54 and 56 'The Second Course'

Lord Peter Wimsey, having seen the front axle of the Daimler taken down and decided that Mr Brownlow and Mr Wilderspin could probably fix it up between them, dispatched his message from the post-office, sent a wire to the friends who were expecting him at Walbeach, and then cast about him for some occupation. The village presented nothing of interest, so he determined to go and have a look at the church. The tolling of the bell had ceased and Hezekiah had gone home; the south door was, however, open, and entering, he discovered Mrs Venables putting fresh water in the altar vases. Catching sight of him as he stood gazing at the exquisite oak tracery of the screen, she came forward to greet him.

'It *is* beautiful, isn't it? Theodore is so proud of his church. And he's done a lot, since we've been here, to keep it looking nice. Fortunately the man before us was conscientious and did his repairs properly, but he was *very* Low and allowed all manner of things that quite shocked us. This beautiful chapel, for instance, would you *believe* that he allowed it to be used for furnace-coke? Of course, we had all that cleared out. Theodore would like a lady-altar here, but we're afraid the parishioners would think it popish. Yes – it's a magnificent window, isn't it? Later than the rest, of course, but so fortunate that it's kept its old glass. We were so afraid when the Zeppelins came over. You know, they dropped a bomb at Walbeach, only twenty miles off, and it might just as easily have been here. Isn't the parclose lovely? Like lace, I always think. The tombs belong to the Gaudy family. They lived here up to Queen Elizabeth's time, but they've all died out now. You'll find the name on the Treble bell: GAUDE, GAUDY, DOMINI IN LAUDE. There used to be a chantry on the north side, corresponding to this: Abbot Thomas' chantry, it was, and that's his tomb. Batty Thomas is named after him – a corruption of 'Abbot,' of course.

NT pp. 56–7 'The Second Course'

He spent the first few minutes after the good lady had left him in putting a suitable donation into the alms-box and in examining the font, whose carvings were certainly curious and, to his mind, suggestive of a symbolism neither altogether Christian nor altogether inocent. He noted a heavy old cope-chest beneath the tower, which, on being opened, proved to contain nothing more venerable than a quantity of worn bell-ropes, and passed on into the north aisle, noticing that the corbels supporting the principals of the angel-roof were very appropriately sculptured with cherubs' heads. He brooded for a little time over the tomb of Abbot Thomas, with its robed and mitred effigy. A stern old boy, he thought, this fourteenth-century cleric, with his strong, harsh face, a ruler rather than a shepherd of his people. Carved panels decorated the sides of the tomb, and showed various scenes in the life of the abbey; one of them depicted the casting of a bell, no doubt of 'Batty Thomas', and it was evident that the Abbot had taken particular pride in his bell, for it appeared again, supporting his feet, in place of the usual cushion. Its decorations and mottoes were realistically rendered: on the shoulder: + NOLI + ESSE + INCREDVLVS + SED + FIDELIS +; on the sound-bow: + *Abbat Thomas sett mee heare* + *and bad mee ringe both lovd and cleer* + 1380 +; and on the waist: O SANCTE THOMA, which inscription, being embellished with an abbot's mitre, left the spectator in a pleasing uncertainty whether the sanctity was to be attributed to the Apostle or the ecclesiastic. It was as well that Abbot Thomas had died long before the spoliation of his house by King Henry. Thomas would have made a fight for it, and his church might have suffered in the process. His successor, douce man, had meekly acquiesced in the usurpation, leaving his abbey to moulder to decay, and his church to be purified peaceably by the reformers. So, at least, the Rector informed Wimsey over the shepherd's pie at lunch.

NT pp. 59–60 'The Second Course'

The voice of the bells of Fenchurch St Paul: Gaude, Gaudy, Domini in laude. Sanctus, sanctus, sanctus Dominus Deus Sabaoth. John Cole made me, John Presbyter paid me, John Evangelist aid me. From Jericho to John a-Groate there is no bell can better my note. Jubilate Deo. Nunc Dimittis, Domine. Abbot Thomas set me here and bad me ring both loud and clear. Paul is my name; honour that same.

Gaude, Sabaoth, John, Jericho, Jubilee, Dimity, Batty Thomas and Tailor Paul.

Nine Tailors Make a Man

NT p. 351 'The Third Part'

Thou shalt pronounce this hideous thing
With cross, and candle, and bell-knelling.

JOHN MYRC: *Instructions for
Parish Priests (15th century)*

Spring and Easter came late together that year to Fenchurch St
Paul. In its own limited, austere and almost grudging fashion the
Fen acknowledged the return of the sun. The floods withdrew
from the pastures: the wheat lifted its pale green spears more
sturdily from the black soil; the stiff thorns bordering dyke
and grass verge budded to a softer outline; on the willows, the
yellow catkins danced like little bell-rope sallies, and the silvery
pussies plumped themselves for the children to carry to church on
Palm Sunday; wherever the grim banks were hedge-sheltered, the
shivering dog-violets huddled from the wind.

In the Rectory garden the daffodils were (in every sense of the
word) in full blow, for in the everlasting sweep and torment of
wind that sweeps across East Anglia, they tossed desperately and
madly. 'My poor daffodils!' Mrs Venables would exclaim, as the
long leaf-tufts streamed over like blown water, and the golden
trumpets kissed the ground, 'this dreadful old wind! I don't know
how they stand it!' She felt both pride and remorse as she cut them
– sound stock varieties, Emperor, Empress, Golden Spur – and
took them away to fill the altar-vases and the two long, narrow
green-painted tin troughs that on Easter Sunday stood one on
either side of the chancel screen. 'The yellow looks so bright,'
thought Mrs Venables, as she tried to persuade the blossoms to
stand upright among the glossy green of periwinkle and St John's
Wort, 'though it really seems a shame to sacrifice them.'

She knelt before the screen on a long red cushion, borrowed
from a pew-seat to protect her 'bones' from the chill of the stone
floor. The four brass altar-vases stood close beside her, in company with the trug full of flowers and a watering-can. Had she
tried to fell them at the Rectory and carry them over, the
sou'wester would have blown them into ruin before she had
so much as crossed the road. 'Tiresome things!' muttered
Mrs Venables, as the daffodils flopped sideways, or slid down
helplessly out of sight into the bottom of the trough.

NT pp. 67–8 'The First Part'

Richard of Chichester

Saints come in all varieties. The only kind that seems to be rare in real life is the spineless and 'goody-goody' figure familiar to us in the feebler sort of pious fiction and stained-glass windows of the more regrettable periods. There are as many types of saint as of men and women, and most of them are people of great character. There are stormy and complex souls like Augustine of Hippo, with his burning sense of sin and his passionate love and dread of physical beauty, pouring out treatises, sermons, memoirs, apologetics, amid the distracting cares of a busy bishopric, travelling for ever between the city of the world and the City of God. There are anchorites, fleeing this world altogether, and devoting themselves to solitude and prayer: some, sweet and gentle like the desert Fathers; some, harsh and fanatical like Simeon Stylites, perched in austere discomfort upon his pillar. There is Francis, the 'troubadour of God', going barefoot among poor men and singing out his love to God and man and the whole creation: there is Albertus Magnus, toiling conscientiously at his vast commentaries upon Aristotle – certainly no singer, but the conspicuous glory of the Schools. There is Albertus's still greater pupil, Thomas Aquinas, a man to whom virtue seemed to come naturally, whose towering intellect completed his master's work and co-ordinated Greek learning and Christian revelation into a comprehensive system of Catholic doctrine: there are some of the companions of S. Francis, whose natural virtue was so naïve that they seem almost 'naturals' in another sense of the word. There is little Theresa of Lisieux, meekly practising the Way amid the trivial duties of daily life and in the face of cramping family opposition: there is mighty Theresa of Avila, the eagle of contemplation, ruling her nuns with that fierce practical ability in which great mystics so often excel, and quite prepared to take God to task, with a tongue as vigorous as Job's and a good deal tarter, when He moved in ways more exasperatingly mysterious than usual. Stubborn martyrs, subtle theologians, ardent missionaries, cloistered contemplatives, homely pastors, brilliant administrators, obscure social workers, orators whose spell-binding eloquence could move multitudes and shake the thrones of princes, the saints seem to have little in common except a heroic love of God and a flaming single-mindedness of purpose.

S. Richard of Chichester . . . is the kind of saint, I think, to appeal strongly to the average English person in whose eyes the mystical fervours of a S. John of the Cross may appear a little morbid, the ascetic rigours of a S. Anthony a little self-centred, the intellectuality of an Aquinas arid and overwhelming. He worked with his hands in the open air; he was unselfishly devoted to his family; he pursued learning with unostentatious industry, and turned that learning to sound practical use; he loved order and seemliness in Church affairs; he was pleasant and familiar with his flock; he had modesty and a sense of humour. The people who, after his death, demanded his canonization probably did so on the simple grounds that, 'Our bishop was such a good man.' So he was: plain and good, like bread; a kind, humble steadfast, cheerful man, courageous under misfortune, just and reasonable in the exercise of authority. Of such is the Kingdom of Heaven.

He loved his people and was beloved by them. He seems to have had no enemies, except King Henry III – a man by whom it was an honour to be disliked. He had a skilled hand with fig trees – that incalculable plant whose fruit, when you can persuade it to bear, tastes so much better in England than anywhere else. As a farmer, he presumably liked horses – at any rate, he was the patron of the Coachmen's Guild of Milan; a fact which bears testimony to the astonishing catholicity of the Middle Ages, when the nations of Europe exchanged their spiritual treasures more generously than they do now, when the common Faith had not yet been split into sects or the common latinity into Babel. The twentieth-century pilgrim might profitably reflect at the shrine of S. Richard on the rich variety of holiness and the reciprocity of gifts. Saints are not all cut to one pattern: they set the innumerable patterns by which the robe of glory may be fashioned. England may be proud to have produced, and lent to her neighbours, a pattern so dignified, so honest, and so becoming as that of S. Richard of Chichester.

Introduction to *Richard of Chichester* by C. M. Duncan-Jones (1953)

3

THE DRAMA OF
THE SOUL'S CHOICE

=

Dorothy Sayers had made her own attempts to understand 'the drama of the soul's choice' in two pre-war Cathedral plays *The Zeal of Thy House* (1937) and *The Devil to Pay* (1939). In this series of extracts from her work, the selections from the second of the two appear first, because *Zeal* is the play to which she later refers in her own essays in self-interpretation with particular reference to her own work as a writer and teacher of the Christian tradition. Just as she was firm in her instructions to the producer of *He That Should Come*, she was also generous in her acknowledgement of the degree to which she depended on the performers of her plays. Her lines 'To the Interpreter' acknowledge the dependence of the creator on the performance of those who will mediate his or her characters to the audience, one giving and receiving from the other in mutuality.

To the Interpreter

'What I have done is yours; what I have to do is
yours; being part in all I have, devoted yours.'

Sound without ear is but an airy stirring,
Light without eyes, but an obscure vibration,
Souls' conference, solitude, and no conferring,
Till it by senses find interpretation;
Gold is not wealth but by the gift and taking,
Speech without mind is only passing vapour;
So is the play, save by the actor's making,
No play, but dull, deaf, senseless ink and paper.

Either for either made: light, eye; sense, spirit;
Ear, sound; gift, gold; play, actor; speech and knowing,
Become themselves by what themselves inherit
From their sole heirs, receiving and bestowing;
Thus, then, do thou, taking what thou dost give,
Live in these lines, by whom alone they live.

DP p. 107

In her introductory observations on what she was attempting to do in re-working the legend of Faustus, Dorothy Sayers thought that as a poet she was dealing with 'the eternities'.

. . . For at the base of it all lies the question of all questions: the nature of Evil and its place in the universe. Symbolise Evil, and call it the Devil, and then ask how the Devil comes to be. Is he, as the Manichees taught, a power co-equal with and opposed to God? Or, if God is all-powerful, did he make the Devil, and if so, why, and with what justification? Is the Devil a positive force, or merely a negation, the absence of Good? In what sense can a man be said to sell his soul to the Devil? What kind of man might do so, and, above all, for what inducement? Further, what meaning are we to place upon the concept of hell and damnation, with which the whole concept of the Devil is intimately bound up?

Questions such as these are answered by every generation in the light of its own spiritual needs and experience. And for each writer, when he has determined his own interpretation of the central mythus, there is, of course, the added technical interest of discovering how many features of the original legend offer themselves as valuable factors in his system of symbolism.

DP Preface, p. 111

On writing *The Devil to Pay*

To endeavour to do again what greater poets have already magnificently done would be folly as well as presumption; and I have tried to offer a new presentment of Faustus. All other considerations apart, I do not feel that the present generation of English people needs to be warned against the passionate pursuit of knowledge for its own sake: that is not our besetting sin. Looking with the eyes of today upon that legendary figure of the man who bartered away his soul, I see in him the type of the impulsive reformer, over-sensitive to suffering, impatient of the facts, eager to set the world right by a sudden overthrow, in his own strength and regardless of the ineluctable nature of things. When he finds it is not to be done, he falls into despair (or, to use the current term, into 'defeatism') and takes flight into phantasy.

His escape takes a form very common in these times: it is the nostalgia of childhood, of the primitive, of the unconscious; the rejection of adult responsibility and the denial of all value to growth and time. Time has been exercising the minds of many writers of late. It has been suggested that it is pure illusion, or at most a cross-section of eternity, and that we may be comforted for the failures of our manhood by remembering that the youthful idealists we once were are our permanent and eternal selves. This doctrine is not really even consoling; since, if our youth is co-eternal with our age, then equally, our age is co-eternal with our youth; the corruptions of our ends poison our beginnings as certainly as the purity of our beginnings sanctifies our ends. The Church has always carefully distinguished the Logos from the Father. It is true that we must become as little children and that 'except a man be born again, he cannot see the kingdom of God.' But that is not to be done by attempting to turn time backwards, or deny its validity in a material universe. 'How can a man be born when he is old? Can he enter the second time into his mother's womb and be born?' The answer is that he cannot. 'That which is born of the flesh is flesh, and that which is born of the spirit is spirit.' Time and eternity are two different things, and that which exists temporally must admit the values of time. Against the exhortation to take refuge in infantilism we may set the saying of Augustine of Hippo concerning Christ: '*Cibus sum grandium;*

38

cresce et manducabis Me' – 'I am the food of the full-grown; become adult, and thou shalt feed on Me.'*

Has Evil any real existence, viewed *sub specie aeternitatis*? I have suggested that it has not; but that it is indissolubly linked with the concept of value in the material and temporal aspect of the universe. It is this issue which Faustus refuses to face; rather than grapple with the opposition of good and evil, he dissociates himself from common human experience. The results to his soul of this attempt to escape reality are displayed in a final judgement scene, where (with a rigid legal exactitude which, I feel sure, the Mediaeval mind would heartily approve) the Devil is cheated of his bond, but receives his precise due. The notion of the Devil as being set in charge of the place of purgation, as well as of the place in which all evil is consumed, was familiar enough to the Middle Ages, as is clearly seen in the Wakefield Pageant of *The Harrowing of Hell*, where Christ rebukes Satan in the words:

> *'I make no mastry but for myne,*
> *I wille theym save, that shalle the sow*
> *Thou hast no powere theym to pyne*
> *Bot in my pryson for thare prow [profit].'*

DP Preface, pp. 112–14

---

* See Hebrews 5:13–14; Augustine's *Confessions* vii, 10; and Dorothy L. Sayers, *Strong Meat* (Hodder & Stoughton, 1939). [Compiler's note]

The temptation of Faustus

FAUSTUS
What? did God make thee? Was all the evil in the world made by God? Beware what thou sayest; I know thee for a false and lying spirit.

MEPHISTOPHELES
That is a most unjust accusation. What lies have I ever told? There is no need for lying, seeing that mankind are such fools.

FAUSTUS
How so?

MEPHISTOPHELES
Why, tell them the truth and they will mislead themselves by their own vanities and save me the trouble of invention. I sat by Eve's shoulder in the shadow of the forbidden tree. 'Eat,' said I, 'and you shall become like God.' She and her silly husband ate, and it was so. Where was the lie? Was it my fault if they persuaded themselves that God was everything they hankered to be – all-good, all-wise, all-powerful and possessed of everlasting happiness?

FAUSTUS
Is not God all these things?

MEPHISTOPHELES
Is He these things? Look at the world He made, and ask yourself, what is He like that made it? Would you not say it was the work of a mad brain, cruel and blind and stupid – this world where the thorn chokes the flower, where the fox slays the fowl and the kite the fox, where the cat torments the mouse for pastime before she kills it for sport? Where men, made truly enough in the image of their Maker, rend, ravish and torture one another, lay waste the earth, burn up provinces for a title or a handful of dirty metal, persecute for a pater-noster, and send a fellow-fool to the rack for the shape of his nose or the name of his mother's father? War, fire, famine, pestilence – is He all-good that delights in these, or all-powerful that likes them not and endures them? Ask thyself this.

FAUSTUS
I have asked it a hundred times without thy prompting. It is as though my own heart spoke to me. Man's cruelty is an abomination – but how can one justify the cruelty of God?

MEPHISTOPHELES
Is He all-wise, that had not the wits to keep out of the mess He had made, but must needs meddle with this business of being a man, and so left matters worse than He found them? Why, He could not even speak His mind plainly, but all He said was so fumblingly expressed, men have been by the ears ever since, trying to make out His meaning. And was not that a prime piece of folly, to show up His nature thus – base and ignorant as any carpenter's son, too poor in spirit to argue in His own defence, too feeble to save His own skin from the hangman? Everlasting happiness? What happiness do you find in the history of the Man of Sorrows? By their fruits ye shall know them.

FAUSTUS
It was He that said that.

MEPHISTOPHELES
So He did, in one of His more unguarded moments.

DP Scene I, pp. 131–3

41

Faustus' rebellion

O, power is grateful to the heart – to change
Sorrow to happiness in a twinkling – blot
The word 'Despair' out of life's lexicon,
And make joy blossom in the desert sand.
Bring me swift horses – bring me the wings of the wind!
We'll fly to the wide world's four distracted corners
Like a great gust of laughter, scattering delight.
We'll do – what will we not do, Mephistopheles?
We will forget old sins – we'll break the cross,
Tear the usurper Christ from His dark throne
And this time bury Him deep and well, beyond
All hope of resurrection.

DP Scene I p. 140

CROWD (*falling to their knees*)
The Holy Father!

FAUSTUS
Stand, then, old man, and hear what I would spit
Into God's teeth, were we set face to face
Even in the Courts of Heaven. God's heart is evil,
Vengeful and tyrannous. He hates the flesh,
The sweet flesh that He made; He treads down beauty
In the winepress of His wrath, pashing it out
To the sour wine of sacrifice; His eye
Is jaundiced to behold such happiness
As men may snatch out of a tortured world.
Look on the symbol in thy hand – the sceptre
Thou rul'st with in His name – it is the yardstick,
The very measure of the devilish hatred
He bears to man, were man His very Son.
Men! I stand here for man, and in man's name

   He springs upon the POPE *and snatches the crucifix from him.*

Defy God's rule, break His accursed sceptre
And smite His regent down.

DP Scene II p. 154

43

FAUSTUS
I too love men; but they are all against me.
They hug their chains; the sacrificial iron
Cankers them at the core. I am not afraid
To suffer; for their sakes I would be damned
Willingly, so I first might do away
Suffering for ever from the pleasant earth.
And here stands power, like a smooth engine, ready
For good or ill alike. Being powerful,
I might be happy – might I not be happy? –
But still the cry of the poor is in my ears
Intolerably. (*To the* POPE): You they call Holy Father –
A kind, compassionate title, 'Holy Father' –
Will you be blind to truth? God, having power,
Uses it like a devil; if He were good
He would turn back the ruthless wheel of time
To the golden age again. I am not God,
But can command the devil's power to serve
Good ends. Which is the devil – God, or I?
Do you be judge between us.

POPE
                              O my poor child,
How much unhappiness is in store for thee!
For thou art taken in the toils of God,
That are more delicate than the spider's thread,
More strong than iron; and though thou wander far
As hell from Heaven, His cunning hand shall twitch
The line, and draw thee home. There is no rest
For such as thee, that bear upon their hearts
The brand of God, and, warring against God,
Make war upon themselves. Thou must be patient,
For God is very patient. Dost thou think
I cannot feel thy griefs? I am the Pope,
Set on a tower above the plains of time
To watch how evil is at odds with good,
And to abide the issue, helpless, save
As prayer and wisdom and the grace of God

44

Shall give me strength. Hard it is, very hard,
To travel up the slow and stony road
To Calvary, to redeem mankind; far better
To make but one resplendent miracle,
Lean through the cloud, lift the right hand of power
And with a sudden lightning smite the world perfect.
Yet this was not God's way, Who had the power,
But set it by, choosing the cross, the thorn,
The sorrowful wounds. Something there is, perhaps,
That power destroys in passing, something supreme,
To whose great value in the eyes of God
That cross, that thorn, and those five wounds bear witness.
Son, go in peace; for thou hast sinned through love;
To such sin God is merciful. Not yet
Has thy familiar devil persuaded thee
To that last sin against the Holy Ghost
Which is, to call good evil, evil good.
Only for that is no forgiveness – Not
That God would not forgive all sins there are,
Being what He is; but that this sin destroys
The power to feel His pardon, so that damnation
Is consequence, not vengeance; and indeed
So all damnation is. I will pray for thee.
And you, my children, go home, gird your loins
And light your lamps, beseeching God to bring
His kingdom nearer, in what way He will.

DP Scene II, pp. 155–6

The judgement scene

JUDGE
All things God can do, but this thing He will not;
Unbind the chain of cause and consequence,
Or speed time's arrow backward. When man chose
To know like God, he also chose to be
Judged by God's values. Adam sinned, indeed,
And with him all mankind; and from that sin
God wrought a nobler virtue out for Adam,
And with him, all mankind. No soul can 'scape
That universal kinship and remain
Human – no man; not even God made man.
He, when He hung upon the fatal tree,
Felt all the passion of the world pierce through Him,
Nor shirked one moment of the ineluctable
Load of the years; but from the griefs of time
Wrought out the splendour of His eternity.
There is no waste with God; He cancels nothing
But redeems all.

DP Scene IV, p. 201

JUDGE

Poor, empty vessel whence the wine was spilt,
What shall we do with thee? Listen to judgment.
For this last time, God gives thee back again
The power to choose, weighing the good and evil –
A fearful option; yet no other course
Can justice take, since here thou standest bound
In thine own blood, and no remorse of thine
Can raze one jot or tittle from the law.
Hear, then, the dread alternative of choice;
And first, wilt thou, with that dumb changeling soul,
Incapable alike of hell or heaven,
Wander for evermore between the worlds
Unblest, undamned, unknowing?

FAUSTUS

                    Nor blest nor damned?
Merciful God, what kind of doom is this?

JUDGE

A gentle doom; sorrow shall never touch thee,
Nor pain, nor any question vex thee more;
Yea, though thy loss be wider than the world,
Or than a thousand thousand worlds at once,
Thou shalt not feel nor know it.

FAUSTUS

                    O, what loss?

JUDGE

A loss beyond all loss: to live content
Eternally, and never look on God;
Never behold the wonder of His face
Fiery with victory, bright above the burning
Wings of the cherubim; never to hear the loud
Exultation of trumpets shatter the sky
For the Lamb's marriage-feast; nor drink the wine
Of God; nor feel the glad earth thrill to the tread

47

Of the tall, strong, unresting angels' feet;
Nor know the dream of desire that is beyond
All happiness nor ever more to find
Beauty in sunlight, or the flowery fields,
Or in man's heart; nor ever laugh again.

FAUSTUS
No, no, no, no!

JUDGE
                    Does ignorance not suffice thee?
Wilt thou have knowledge after all, John Faustus?
Take back thy soul, then, and fulfil the bond;
Go down with Mephistopheles to hell,
And through the bars of those relentless gates
Gaze on the glory of the Lord far off
And know that He is terrible and just.

FAUSTUS
No choice but this?

JUDGE
                    No other choice at all.

FAUSTUS
Either to lose God and not know the loss,
Nor even to remember God exists;
Or see the glories that I may not share,
And in the sharp hell of a lost desire
Burn on unquenchably.

JUDGE
                    So stands the choice.

FAUSTUS
O lost, lost, either way!

DP Scene IV, pp. 203–5

Faustus' choice of Christ

FAUSTUS
                    I have chosen.
I will go down with Mephistopheles
To the nethermost pit of fire unquenchable
Where no hope is, and over the pathless gulf
Look up to God. Beyond that gulf I may
Never pass over, nor any saint nor angel
Descend to me. Nevertheless, I know
Whose feet can tread the fire as once the water,
And I will call upon Him out of the deep,
Out of the deep, O Lord.

JUDGE
                    Art now so bold
To call down God, thou that aforetime didst
With cowardly conjurations call up devils?
Then tell me: art thou able to be baptised
With Christ's most bitter baptism, or to drink
The cup that all His shuddering mortal flesh
Shrank from, yet drank, down to the dark dregs, driven
By the strong spirit?

FAUSTUS
                    I dare not say I am able.
Yet I say this: that nothing thou canst do
Shall threat me from the quest of Christ eternal.
Yea, though thou stand with thy keen sword made
    bare
To keep me from Him, and have at thy command
In ninefold rank the terrible hosts of Heaven,
Yet will I seek Him. If I go down to hell
He is there also; or if He stand without,
My hands shall batter against hell's brazen gates
Till the strong bars burst asunder and let Him in.
Then will I seize Him, then fall down before Him,
Cling to His garments, hold Him fast by the feet,
Cry in His ear, 'I will not let Thee go
Except Thou bless me. Even the unjust judge

Heard the poor widow, and Thou shalt hear me!
Spare not Thy rod, for Thou hast borne the rod,
Quench not Thy fire, for Thou didst pass through fire,
Only be with me!'

MEPHISTOPHELES
        This is brave indeed!

FAUSTUS
Mock me not, nothingness; I have found courage
In Him that never feared to look on sorrow,
And though He slay me, I will trust in Him.
. . .

JUDGE
        Faustus, look on me;
Through the harsh mask of judgment read my soul,
And when I meet thee at the gates of hell,
Know me again.

FAUSTUS
        Slay me, but leave me not.

JUDGE
Lo! I will never leave thee, nor forsake thee
Even to the world's end. Take him, Mephistopheles,
And purge him throughly, till he find himself,
As I have found him mine. God is not robbed;
And I will bring mine own as I did sometime
From the deep of the sea again.

                                         DP Scene IV, pp. 208–11

4

THE DOGMA IS
THE DRAMA

=

Canterbury Cathedral under its Dean G. K. Bell had commissioned Eliot's *Murder in the Cathedral* for 1935, and then a play on Cranmer by Charles Williams for 1936. For the Festival or Service of Arts and Crafts in 1937 the invitation came to Dorothy Sayers, and the result was *The Zeal of Thy House* (see Psalm 69:9 and John 2:17). The central theme, of the greatest importance to her personally, was the integrity of one's work and the problem of the artist who neglects God for it, but whose work finally redeems his personal weaknesses when acknowledged as a tribute to the divine creator. I have mentioned already that she would never accept that the 'value' of someone's work could be reduced only to its market value, and this will be a theme that re-emerges in her concern with the values of post-world-war Britain. That apart, we could attribute to Dorothy Sayers herself Harriet's self-evaluation in *Gaudy Night*:

> Was there anything at all that had stood firm in the midst of her indecision? Well, yes, she had stuck to her work — and that in the face of what might have seemed overwhelming reasons for abandoning it and doing something different.

GN ch. II, p. 42

That novel explores the damage that can be done when intellect and emotion are disjoined. Nevertheless, one of its turning points comes when Peter appreciates in Harriet something of the intellectual integrity of the pure scholar. He writes to her that 'I know that, if you have put anything in hand, disagreeableness and danger will not turn you back, and God forbid they should' – an admission of equality she had not expected of him (GN p. 229). Harriet's reply to him thanks him for not telling her to run away and play, her acknowledgement of the best compliment he had ever paid her. This reduces even Peter to silence!

William, the architect of *Zeal*, is Dorothy Sayers too, living between the vindicating justice of God and the envy of Satan, to paraphrase the words of the monk who chronicled both the fire of 1174 and the fate of the man who rebuilt the cathedral. She was to quote some of the words from this play to her son Anthony in a letter of January 2, 1940 (Brabazon p. 163) as a way of expressing her own sense of what she might have achieved. The words come from William's appeal (comparable to Faustus' final choice) in his confession of penitence, 'Let me lie deep in hell,/Death gnaw upon me, purge my bones with fire' so long as his work could stand to God's glory (like that of the makers of the angel-roof which entranced Wimsey in *The Nine Tailors*). When I first read *Zeal* and then her other cathedral plays, I misguidedly supposed that the intensity and complexity of her language reflected the fact that she believed herself to be writing for an audience who knew their classical Christian doctrine. On the contrary, I came to realize, she conceived her plays as works of instruction, and was hardly critically self-aware of the way in which she was filtering the Latin western tradition of Christianity through her own very unusual literary and dramatic talent. Before the end of her life she was to be challenged to recognize that creeds and particular formulations of doctrines themselves had a history, to which she herself was contributing, and that the formulation of belief might change. Not everyone might love the pattern of belief which gave her such ecstatic intellectual satisfaction, but some might require a different pattern addressed to genuinely novel discovery of reality. In the end, though she appreciated that Christian doctrine took some believing, the problem as she saw it was that people simply could not believe that 'anything so interesting, so exciting, and so dramatic can be the orthodox Creed of the Church'.

Revolutionary novelties

That this is really the case was made plain to me by the questions asked me, mostly by young men, about my Canterbury play, *The Zeal of Thy House*. The action of the play involves a dramatic presentation of a few fundamental Christian dogmas – in particular, the application to human affairs of the doctrine of the Incarnation. That the Church believed Christ to be in any *real* sense God, or that the Eternal Word was supposed to be associated in any way with the work of Creation; that Christ was held to be at the same time Man in any *real* sense of the word; that the doctrine of the Trinity could be considered to have any relation to fact or any bearing on psychological truth; that the Church considered Pride to be sinful, or indeed took notice of any sin beyond the more disreputable sins of the flesh: – all these things were looked upon as astonishing and revolutionary novelties, imported into the Faith by the feverish imagination of a playwright. I protested in vain against this flattering tribute to my powers of invention, referring my inquirers to the creeds, to the Gospels, and to the offices of the Church; I insisted that if my play was dramatic it was so, not in spite of the dogma but because of it – that, in short, the dogma *was* the drama. The explanation was, however, not well received; it was felt that if there was anything attractive in Christian philosophy I must have put it there myself.

'The Dogma is the Drama', CC pp. 20–1

Perhaps we are not following Christ all the way or in quite the right spirit. We are apt, for example, to be a little sparing of the palms and the hosannas. We are chary of wielding the scourge of small cords, lest we should offend somebody or interfere with trade. We do not furbish up our wits to disentangle knotty questions about Sunday observance and tribute-money, nor hasten to sit at the feet of the doctors, both hearing them and asking them questions. We pass hastily over disquieting jests about making friends with the mammon of unrighteousness and alarming observations about bringing not peace but a sword; nor do we distinguish ourselves by the graciousness with which we sit at meat with publicans and sinners. Somehow or other, and with the best intentions, we have shown the world the typical Christian in the likeness of a crashing and rather ill-natured bore – and this in the Name of One who assuredly never bored a soul in those thirty-three years during which He passed through the world like a flame.

Let us, in Heaven's name, drag out the Divine Drama from under the dreadful accumulation of slipshod thinking and trashy sentiment heaped upon it, and set it on an open stage to startle the world into some sort of vigorous reaction. If the pious are the first to be shocked, so much the worse for the pious – others will pass into the Kingdom of Heaven before them. If all men are offended because of Christ, let them be offended; but where is the sense of their being offended at something that is not Christ and is nothing like Him? We do Him singularly little honour by watering down His personality till it could not offend a fly. Surely it is not the business of the Church to adapt Christ to men, but to adapt men to Christ.

It is the dogma that is the drama – not beautiful phrases, nor comforting sentiments, nor vague aspirations to loving-kindness and uplift, nor the promise of something nice after death – but the terrifying assertion that the same God who made the world lived in the world and passed through the grave and gate of death. Show that to the heathen, and they may not believe it; but at least they may realize that here is something that a man might be glad to believe.

DD pp. 23–4

The Zeal of Thy House

Behold, he prayeth; not with the lips alone,
But with the hand and with the cunning brain
Men worship the Eternal Architect.
So, when the mouth is dumb, the work shall speak
And save the workman. True as mason's rule
And line can make them, the shafted columns rise
Singing like music; and by day and night
The unsleeping arches with perpetual voice
Proclaim in Heaven, to labour is to pray.

ZH Scene II, p. 38

For our purposes, the plot of *Zeal* is not particularly important, but it may be helpful to know a little about it. William of Sens was chosen by a nervous Cathedral Chapter to reconstruct the choir which had been burnt down. His speech, headed here 'William's Pride', is a preface to his claim that to God he is indispensable for the completion of the work. A flawed rope breaks, William falls from his cradle high up in the scaffolding, is crippled but not killed. Absolved of his 'fleshly faults' he is brought to acknowledge the sin in his work, his pride, and this makes it possible for him to leave the completion of his work to others.

William's pride

We are the master-craftsmen, God and I –
We understand one another. None, as I can,
Can creep under the ribs of God, and feel
His heart beat through those Six Days of Creation;
Enormous days of slowly turning lights
Streaking the yet unseasoned firmament;
Giant days, Titan days, yet all too short
To hold the joy of making. God caught His breath
To see the poles of the world stand up through chaos;
And when He sent it forth, the great winds blew,
Carrying the clouds. And then He made the trees
For winds to rustle through – oak, poplar, cedar
Hawthorn and elm, each with its separate motion –
And with His delicate fingers painted the flowers,
Numberless – numberless! why make so many
But that He loved the work, as I love mine,
And saw that it was good, as I see mine? –
The supple, swift mechanics of the serpent,
The beautiful, furred beasts, and curious fish
With golden eyes and quaintly-laced thin bones,
And whales like mountains loud with spurting springs,
Dragons and monsters in strange shapes, to make
His angels laugh with Him; when He saw those
God sang for joy, and formed the birds to sing.
And lastly, since all Heaven was not enough
To share that triumph, He made His masterpiece,
Man, that like God can call beauty from dust,
Order from chaos, and create new worlds
To praise their maker. Oh, but in making man
God over-reached Himself and gave away
His Godhead. He must now depend on man
For what man's brain, creative and divine
Can give Him. Man stands equal with Him now,
Partner and rival. Say God needs a church,
As here in Canterbury – and say He calls together
By miracle stone, wood and metal, builds
A church of sorts; *my* church He cannot make –
Another, but not that. This church is mine

And none but I, not even God, can build it.
Me hath He made vice-regent of Himself,
And were I lost, something unique were lost
Irreparably; my heart, my blood, my brain
Are in the stone; God's crown of matchless works
Is not complete without my stone, my jewel,
Creation's nonpareil.

ZH Scene III, pp. 67–8

William's controversy with the archangel

WILLIAM
For all that He can do I will not yield,
Nor leave to other men that which is mine,
To botch – to alter – turn to something else,
Not mine.

MICHAEL
       Thou wilt not? Yet God bore this too,
The last, the bitterest, worst humiliation,
Bowing His neck under the galling yoke
Frustrate, defeated, half His life unlived,
Nothing achieved.

WILLIAM
               Could God, being God, do this?

MICHAEL
Christ, being man, did this; but still, through faith
Knew what He did. As gold and diamond,
Weighed in the chemist's balance, are but earth
Like tin or iron, albeit within them still
The purchase of the world lie implicit:
So, when God came to test of mortal time
In nature of a man whom time supplants,
He made no reservation of Himself
Nor of the godlike stamp that franked His gold,
But in good time let time supplant Him too.
The earth was rent, the sun's face turned to blood,
But He, unshaken, with exultant voice
Cried, 'It is finished!' and gave up the ghost.
'Finished' – when men had thought it scarce begun.
Then His disciples with blind faces mourned,
Weeping: 'We trusted that He should redeem
Israel; but now we know not.' What said He
Behind the shut doors in Jerusalem,
At Emmaus, and in the bitter dawn
By Galilee: 'I go; but feed My sheep;
For Me the Sabbath at the long week's close –

For you the task, for you the tongues of fire.'
Thus shalt thou know the Master Architect,
Who plans so well, He may depart and leave
The work to others. Art thou more than God?
Not God Himself was indispensable,
For lo! God died – and still His work goes on.

ZH Scene IV, pp. 97–8

William's confession

O, I have sinned. The eldest sin of all,
Pride, that struck down the morning star from Heaven
Hath struck down me from where I sat and shone
Smiling on my new world. All other sins
God will forgive but that. I am damned, damned,
Justly. Yet, O most just and merciful God,
Hear me but once, Thou that didst make the world
And wilt not let one thing that Thou hast made,
No, not one sparrow, perish without Thy Will
(Since what we make, we love) — for that love's sake
Smite only me and spare my handiwork.
Jesu, the carpenter's Son, the Master-builder,
Architect, poet, maker — by those hands
That Thine own nails have wounded — by the wood
Whence Thou didst carve Thy Cross — let not the Church
Be lost through me. Let me lie deep in hell,
Death gnaw upon me, purge my bones with fire,
But let my work, all that was good in me,
All that was God, stand up and live and grow.
The work is sound, Lord God, no rottenness there —
Only in me. Wipe out my name from men
But not my work; to other men the glory
And to Thy Name alone. But if to the damned
Be any mercy at all, O send Thy spirit
To blow apart the sundering flames, that I
After a thousand years of hell, may catch
One glimpse, only one, of the Church of Christ,
The perfect work, finished, though not by me.

ZH Scene IV, pp. 98–9

MICHAEL

How hardly shall the rich man enter in
To the Kingdom of Heaven! By what sharp, thorny ways,
By what strait gate at last! But when he is come,
The angelic trumpets split their golden throats
Triumphant, to the stars singing together
And all the sons of God shouting for joy.
Be comforted, thou that wast rich in gifts;
For thou art broken on the self-same rack
That broke the richest Prince of all the world,
The Master-man. Thou shalt not surely die,
Save as He died; nor suffer, save with Him;
Nor lie in hell, for He hath conquered hell
And flung the gates wide open. They that bear
The cross with Him, with Him shall wear a crown
Such as the angels know not. Then be still,
And know that he is God, and God alone.

ZH Scene IV, p. 100

MICHAEL

Children of men, Lift up your hearts. Laud and magnify God, the everlasting Wisdom, the holy, undivided and adorable Trinity.

Praise Him that He hath made man in His own image, a maker and craftsman like Himself, a little mirror of His triune majesty.

For every work of creation is threefold, an earthly trinity to match the heavenly.

First: there is the Creative Idea; passionless, timeless, beholding the whole work complete at once, the end in the beginning; and this is the image of the Father.

Second: there is the Creative Energy, begotten of that Idea, working in time from the beginning to the end, with sweat and passion, being incarnate in the bonds of matter; and this is the image of the Word.

Third: there is the Creative Power, the meaning of the work and its response in the lively soul; and this is the image of the indwelling Spirit.

And these three are one, each equally in itself the whole work, whereof none can exist without other; and this is the image of the Trinity.

Behold, then, and honour, all beautiful work of the craftsman, imagined by men's minds, built by the labour of men's hands, working with power upon the souls of men, image of the everlasting Trinity, God's witness in world and time.

And whatsoever ye do, do all to the Glory of God.

ZH Scene IV, pp. 102–3, and author's preface, pp. 11–12

On those words from *The Zeal of Thy House* Dorothy Sayers wrote:

Of these clauses, the one which gives the most trouble to the hearer is that dealing with the Creative Idea. (The word is here used, not in the philosopher's sense, in which the 'Idea' tends to be equated with the 'Word', but quite simply in the sense intended by the writer when he says: 'I have an idea for a book.') The ordinary man is apt to say: 'I thought you began by collecting material and working out the plot.' The confusion here is not merely over the words 'first' and 'begin'. In fact the 'Idea' – or rather the writer's realization of his own idea – does precede any mental or physical work upon the materials or on the course of the story within a time-series. But apart from this, the very formulation of the Idea in the writer's mind is not the Idea itself, but its self-awareness in the Energy. Everything that is conscious, everything that has to do with form and time, and everything that has to do with process, belongs to the working of the Energy or Activity or 'Word'. The Idea, that is, cannot be said to precede the Energy in time, because (so far as that act of creation is concerned) it is the Energy that creates the time-process. This is the analogy of the theological expressions that 'the Word was in the beginning with God' and was 'eternally begotten of the Father'. If, that is, the act has a beginning in time at all, it is because of the presence of the Energy or Activity. The writer cannot even be conscious of his Idea except by the working of the Energy which formulates it to himself.

That being so, how can we know that the Idea itself has any real existence apart from the Energy? Very strangely; by the fact that the Energy itself is conscious of referring all its acts to an existing and complete whole. In theological terms, the Son does the will of the Father. Quite simply, every choice of an episode, or a phrase, or a word is made to conform to a pattern of the entire book, which is revealed by that choice as already existing. This truth, which is difficult to convey in explanation, is quite clear and obvious in experience. It manifests itself plainly enough when the writer says or thinks: 'That is, or is not, the right phrase' – meaning that it is a phrase which does or does not correspond to the reality of the Idea.

Further, although the book – that is, the activity of writing the book – is a process in space and time, it is known to the writer as *also* a complete and timeless whole, 'the end in the beginning', and this knowledge of it is with him always, while writing it and after it is finished, just as it was at the beginning. It is not changed or affected by the toils and troubles of composition, nor is the writer aware of his book as merely a succession of words and situations. The Idea of the book is a thing-in-itself quite apart from its awareness or its manifestation in Energy, though it still remains true that it cannot be known as a thing-in-itself except as the Energy reveals it. The Idea is thus timeless and without parts or passions, though it is never seen, either by writer or reader, except in terms of time, parts and passion.

The Energy itself is an easier concept to grasp, because it is the thing of which the writer is conscious and which the reader can see when it is manifest in material form. It is dynamic – the sum and process of all the activity which brings the book into temporal and spatial existence. 'All things are made by it, and without it nothing is made that has been made.' To it belongs everything that can be included under the word 'passion' – feeling, thought, toil, trouble, difficulty, choice, triumph – all the accidents which attend a manifestation in time. It is the Energy that is the creator in the sense in which the common man understands the word, because it brings about an expression in temporal form of the eternal and immutable Idea. It is, for the writer, what he means by 'the writing of the book', and it includes, though it is not confined to, the manifestation of the book in material form. We shall have more to say about it in the following chapters: for the moment, the thing I am anxious to establish is that it is something distinct from the Idea itself, though it is the only thing that can make the Idea known to itself or to others, and yet is (in the ideal creative act which we are considering) essentially identical with the Idea – 'consubstantial with the Father'.

The Creative Power is the third 'Person' of the writer's trinity. It is not the same thing as the Energy (which for greater clearness I ought perhaps to have called 'the Activity'), though it proceeds from the Idea and the Energy together. It is the thing which flows back to the writer from his own activity and makes him, as it were, the reader of his own book. It is also, of course, the means by which the Activity is communicated to other readers and which produces a corresponding response in them. In fact, from the readers' point of view, it *is* the book. By it, they perceive the book, both as a process in time and as an eternal whole, and react to it dynamically. It is at this point we begin to understand what St. Hilary means in saying of the Trinity: 'Eternity is in the Father, form in the Image and use in the Gift.'

Lastly: 'these three are one, each equally in itself the whole work, whereof none can exist without other.' If you were to ask a writer which is 'the real book' – his Idea of it, his Activity in writing it or its return to himself in Power, he would be at a loss to tell you, because these things are essentially inseparable. Each of them is the complete book separately; yet in the complete book all of them exist together. He can, by an act of the intellect, 'distinguish the persons' but he cannot by any means 'divide the substance'. How could he? He cannot know the Idea, except by the Power interpreting his own Activity to him; he knows the Activity only as it reveals the Idea in Power; he knows the Power only as the revelation of the Idea in the Activity. All he can say is that these three are equally and eternally present in his own act of creation, and at every moment of it, whether or not the act ever becomes manifest in the form of a written and printed book. These things are not confined to the material manifestation: they exist in – they *are* – the creative mind itself.

'Idea, Energy, Power', MM pp. 28–31

Pentecost

When the writer's Idea is revealed or incarnate by his Energy, then, and only then, can his Power work on the world. More briefly and obviously, a book has no influence till somebody can read it.

Before the Energy was revealed or incarnate it was, as we have seen, already present in Power within the creator's mind, but now that Power is released for communication to other men, and returns from their minds to his with a new response. It dwells in them and works upon them with creative energy, producing in them fresh manifestations of Power.

This is the Power of the Word, and it is dangerous. Every word – even every idle word – will be accounted for at the day of judgment, because the word itself has power to bring to judgment. It is of the nature of the word to reveal itself and to incarnate itself – to assume material form. Its judgment is therefore an intellectual, but also a material judgment. The habit, very prevalent to-day, of dismissing words as 'just words' takes no account of their power. But once the Idea has entered into other minds, it will tend to reincarnate itself there with ever-increasing Energy and ever-increasing Power. It may for some time only incarnate itself in more words, more books, more speeches; but the day comes when it incarnates itself in actions, and this is its day of judgment. At the time when these words are being written, we are witnessing a fearful judgment of blood, resulting from the incarnation in deeds of an Idea to which, when it was content with a verbal revelation, we paid singularly little heed. Which Ideas are (morally) Good and which are anti-Good it is not the purpose of this book to discuss; what is now abundantly manifest is the Power. Any Idea whose Energy manifests itself in a Pentecost of Power is good from its own point of view. It shows itself to be a true act of creation, although, if it is an evil Idea, it will create to a large extent by active negation – that is to say, by destruction. The fact, however, that 'all activity is of God' means that no creative Idea can be wholly destructive: some creation will be produced together with the destruction; and it is the work of the creative mind to see that the destruction is redeemed by its creative elements.

It is the business of education to wait upon Pentecost. Unhappily, there is something about educational syllabuses, and especially about examination papers, which seems to be rather out of

67

harmony with Pentecostal manifestations. The Energy of Ideas does not seem to descend into the receptive mind with quite that rush of cloven fire which we ought to expect. Possibly there is something lacking in our Idea of education; possibly something inhibiting has happened to the Energy. But Pentecost will happen, whether within or without official education. From some quarter or other, the Power will descend, to flame or to smoulder until it is ready to issue in a new revelation. We need not suppose that, because the mind of the reader is inert to Plato, it will therefore be inert to Nietzsche or Karl Marx; failing those, it may respond to Wilhelmina Stitch or to Hollywood. No incarnate Idea is altogether devoid of Power; if the Idea is feeble, the Energy dispersed, and the Power dim, the indwelling spirit will be dim, dispersed and feeble – but such as it is, so its response will be and such will be its manifestation in the world.

It is through the Power that we get a reflection in the mind of the world of the original Trinity in the mind of the writer. For the reader, that is, the book itself is presented as a threefold being.

First: the Book as Thought – the Idea of the book existing in the writer's mind. Of this, the reader can be aware only by faith. He knows that it does exist, but it is unknowable to him except in its manifestations. He can, of course, suppose if he likes that the book corresponds to nothing at all in the writer's mind; he can, if he likes, think that it got into its visible form by accident and that there is not and never was any such person as the writer. He is perfectly free to think these things, though in practice he seldom avails himself of this freedom. Where a book is concerned, the average man is a confirmed theist. There was, certainly, a little time ago, a faint tendency to polytheism among the learned. In particular cases, that is, where there was no exterior evidence about the writer, the theory was put forward that the *Iliad*, for example, and the *Song of Roland* were written by 'the folk'; some extremists actually suggested that they 'just happened' – though even such people were forced to allow the mediation of a little democracy of godlets to account for the material form in which these manifestations presented themselves. To-day, the polytheistic doctrine is rather at a discount; at any rate it is generally conceded that the Energy exhibited in written works must have emanated from some kind of Idea in a personal mind.

Secondly: the Book as Written – the Energy or Word incarnate, the express image of the Idea. This is the book that stands upon our shelves, and everything within and about it: characters, episodes, the succession of words and phrases, style, grammar, paper and ink, and, of course, the story itself. The incarnation of the Energy stands wholly within the space-time frame: it is written by a material pen and printed by a material machine upon material paper; the words were produced as a succession of events succeeding one another in time. Any timelessness, illimitability or uncreatedness which may characterise the book belongs not here but in the mind; the *body* of the Energy is a created thing, strictly limited by time and space, and subject to any accident that may befall matter. If we do not like it, we are at liberty to burn it in the market-place, or subject it to any other indignity, such as neglecting it, denying it, spitting upon it, or writing hostile reviews about it. We must, however, be careful to see that nobody reads it before we take steps to eliminate it; otherwise, it may disconcert us by rising again – either as a new Idea in somebody's mind, or even (if somebody has a good memory) in a resurrected body, substantially the same though made of new materials. In this respect, Herod showed himself much more competent and realistic than Pilate or Caiaphas. He grasped the principle that if you are to destroy the Word, you must do so before it has time to communicate itself. Crucifixion gets there too late.

Thirdly: the Book as Read – the Power of its effect upon and in the responsive mind. This is a very difficult thing to examine and analyse, because our own perception of the thing is precisely what we are trying to perceive. We can, as it were, note various detached aspects of it: what we cannot pin down and look at is the movement of our own mind. In the same way, we cannot follow the movement of our own eyes in a mirror. We can, by turning our head, observe them in this position and in that position with respect to our body, but never in the act of moving themselves from one position to the other, and never in the act of gazing at anything but the mirror. Thus our idea of ourself is bound to be falsified, since what to others appears the most lively and mobile part of ourself, appears to us unnaturally fixed. The eye is the instrument by which we see everything, and for that reason it is the one thing we cannot see with truth. The same thing is true of our Power of response to a book, or to anything else; incidentally, this is why books about the Holy Ghost are apt to be curiously difficult and unsatisfactory – we cannot really look at the movement of the Spirit, just because It is the Power by which we do the looking.

'Pentecost', MM pp. 88–91

So, on *The Nine Tailors*:

It is interesting to rake into one's own mind and discover, if one can, what were the combined sources of power on which one, consciously or unconsciously, drew while endeavouring to express an idea in writing. Here, for instance, is a whole string of familiar passages which were obviously hovering about in my memory when I wrote a phrase in *The Nine Tailors*.

When the morning stars sang together, and all the sons of God shouted for joy.

Book of Job

Above it stood the seraphims: each one had six wings; with twain he covered his face, and with twain he covered his feet, and with twain he did fly.

Book of the Prophet Isaiah

He rode upon the cherubims and did fly; He came flying upon the wings of the wind.

Psalms of David

With Saintly shout and solemn Jubily,
Where the bright Seraphim in burning row
Their loud up-lifted Angel trumpets blow,
And the Cherubick host in thousand quires
Touch their immortal Harps of golden wires,
With those just Spirits that wear victorious Palms,
Hymns devout and holy Psalms
Singing everlastingly.

Milton: *At a Solemn Musick*

The carved angels, ever eager-eyed,
Stand, where upon their heads the cornice rests,

70

With hair blown back, and wings put cross-wise on their
breasts.

Keats: *The Eve of St Agnes*

Only they see not God, I know,
Nor all that chivalry of His,
The soldier-saints who, row on row,
Burn upward each to his point of bliss.

Browning: *The Statue and the Bust*

. . . incredibly aloof, flinging back the light in a dusky shimmer
of bright hair and gilded outspread wings, soared the ranked
angels, cherubim and seraphim, choir over choir, from corbel
and hammer-beam floating face to face uplifted.

The Nine Tailors

In addition to the passages quoted, there is, of course, the direct
association with actual angel-roofs, such as that in March Parish
Church, which I know well, and pictures of others, such as that at
Needham Market. Vaguely, too, I fancy, there was an echo of
other, remoter associations:

. . . all the dim rich city, roof by roof,
Tower after tower, spire beyond spire,
By grove and garden-lawn and rushing brook,
Climbs to the mighty hall that Merlin built.
And four great zones of sculpture, set betwixt
With many a mystic symbol, gird the hall:
And in the lowest, beasts are slaying men,
And in the second, men are slaying beasts,
And on the third are warriors, perfect men,
And on the fourth are men with growing wings,
And over all one statue in the mould
Of Arthur, made by Merlin, with a crown,
And peaked wings pointed to the Northern Star.

Tennyson: *The Holy Grail*

Four great figures the corners on,
Matthew and Mark and Luke and John.

Camilla Doyle (a poem read years ago, the title
of which I have quite forgotten. This is itself
'associated' with the children's rhyme about
Matthew, Mark, Luke and John).

Where the walls
of Magnus Martyr hold
Inexplicable splendour of Ionian white and gold.

T. S. Eliot: The Waste Land

A bracelet of bright hair about the bone.

John Donne: The Funeral

It is of course, open to anyone to point out that these great streams of power have been much diminished by pouring through my narrow channel. That is quite true, and is partly a measure of my lack of capacity and partly a recognition of the fact that any passage within a work demands a volume of power appropriate to its place in the unity of that work and no more. But what is important, and not always understood in these days, is that a reminiscent passage of this kind is *intended* to recall to the reader all the associated passages, and so put him in touch with the sources of power behind and beyond the writer. The demand for 'originality' – with the implication that the reminiscence of other writers is a sin against originality and a defect in the work – is a recent one and would have seemed quite ludicrous to poets of the Augustan Age, or of Shakespeare's time. The traditional view is that each new work should be a fresh focus of power through which former streams of beauty, emotion, and reflection are directed. This view is adopted, and perhaps carried to excess, by writers like T. S. Eliot, some of whose poems are a close web of quotations and adaptations, chosen for their associative value, or like James Joyce, who makes great use of the associative value of sounds and syllables. The criterion is, not whether the associations are called up, but whether the spirits invoked by this kind of verbal incantation are charged with personal power by the magician who speeds them about their new business.

The Power – the Spirit – is thus a social power, working to bring all minds into its own unity, sometimes by similarity and at other times by contrast. There is a diversity of gifts, but the same spirit. Sometimes we feel that a critic or student of a man's work has 'read into it' a good deal more than the first writer 'meant'. This is, perhaps, to have a rather confined apprehension of the unity and diversity of the Power. In the narrower sense, it is doubtless true that when Solomon or somebody wrote the *Song of Songs* he did not 'mean' to write an epithalamium on the mystic nuptials of

Christ with His Church. By the same process of reasoning, when Drayton wrote:

> Since there's no help, come, let us kiss and part;
> Nay, I have done: You get no more of me ...

he did not *mean* to express the complicated emotion of impatience, relief, acceptance and forlorn hope which *you* experienced 'at the last gasp of Love's latest breath'. Nevertheless, he was a true prophet of your emotion, since he *did* express it, so that you feel the lines to have been written 'for you'. In coming into contact with his Power, through the ink-and-paper body of his Energy, you are taken up into the eternal unity of Drayton's Idea. You now lie within the orbit of the Power, which (immanent and transcendent) is also within you, and your response to it will bring forth further power, according to your own capacity and energy. If you react to it creatively, your response will again assume the form of: an Idea in your mind, the manifestation of that Idea in some form of Energy or Activity (speech, behaviour or what not), and a communication of Power to the world about you.

This threefoldness in the reader's mind corresponds to the threefoldness of the work (Book-as-Thought, Book-as-Written, Book-as-Read), and that again to the original threefoldness in the mind of the writer (Idea, Energy, Power). It is bound to be so, because that is the structure of the creative mind. When, therefore, we consider Trinitarian doctrine about the universal Creator, this is what we are driving at. We are arguing on the analogy of something perfectly familiar to our experience. The implication is that we find the threefold structure in ourselves (the-Book-as-Read) because that is the actual structure of the universe (the-Book-as-Written), and that it is in the universe because it is in God's Idea about the universe (the-Book-as-Thought); further, that this structure is in God's Idea because it is the structure of God's mind.

This is what the doctrine *means*; whether it is true or mistaken is another matter, but this is the Idea that is put forward for our response. There is nothing mythological about Christian Trinitarian doctrine: it is analogical.

'Pentecost', MM pp. 94–8

5

THE MIND OF
THE MAKER

=

That explanation of what she was up to in *Zeal* and *The Nine Tailors* comes from Dorothy Sayers' unjustly neglected *The Mind of the Maker* of 1941, important not merely for the development of a Christian aesthetic in these days when it is far from clear that Christians are capable of praising artistic excellence, but for an understanding of the experience of freedom and love by a creative artist in respect of her own work. Some of her characteristic arguments on this latter theme can also be found in her contribution to the conference held in Malvern in 1941, where she claimed

> that the divine Beauty is sovereign within His own dominion; and that if a statue is ill-carved or a play ill-written, the artist's corruption is deeper than if the statue were obscene and the play blasphemous. Deeper, because the artist is being false to his own vision of the Truth; because it is a sapping from within of that disinterested integrity which is the point at which men can touch the Truth that is outside space and time.

> (ML p. 75)

In *The Mind of the Maker* we have a text which could well have been expected from the pen of a theologian with an ecclesiastical or institutional base of some kind, but she claimed, as always, to write 'as a professional writer', though she has a wry comment to make on this in the Preface to *The Mind of the Maker*: 'If one must use this curious expression. The theory that what writes is not the self but some aspect of the self is popular these days. It assists pigeon-holing. It

is, of course, heretical – a form of Sabellianism no doubt . . .'
(MM Preface, p. x note).

She tests writers by correlating classical heresies with their artistic parallels, and such correlation undoubtedly has its dangers as well as its amusing side. One danger is the threat of destroying precisely that disinterested integrity about which she was so eloquent. For an artist who happened to be an articulate Christian might foster a preoccupation with 'orthodoxy' in her or himself at the possible expense of simply writing the good play or detective story, or carving a statue or whatever. Another danger might be to place beyond criticism those artists whose work *did* survive the criteria of orthodoxy, as Dante's undoubtedly did for her. Still, she is to be commended for wanting a 'sacramental' view of creative freedom and talent, the human somehow giving us clues to the divine, clear that the artist is subject to the judgement of God and must not misuse his materials or regard himself as their creator. The core of her position can be identified in the deceptively simple claim that to let ourselves be spoonfed with the ready-made is to lose our grip on our only true life and our only real selves (UO p. 18).

The Mind of the Maker was written when she had given up writing detective fiction and could reflect on her own achievements and what they meant to her, in line with those statements in the creeds of Christendom which purport to be statements of fact. She was not concerned at this juncture with those statements which are historical, but with those which are theological, that is, about the nature of God and the universe, drawn up under a sense of urgent and practical necessity.

Theological statements

In the creeds of Christendom, we are confronted with a set of documents which purport to be, not expressions of opinion but statements of fact. Some of these statements are historical, and with these the present book is not concerned. Others are theological – which means that they claim to be statements of fact about the nature of God and the universe; and with a limited number of these I propose to deal.

The selected statements are those which aim at defining the nature of God, conceived in His capacity as Creator. They were originally drawn up as defences against heresy – that is, specifically to safeguard the fact against opinions which were felt to be distortions of fact. It will not do to regard them as the product of irresponsible speculation, spinning fancies for itself in a vacuum. That is the reverse of the historical fact about them. They would never have been drawn up at all but for the urgent practical necessity of finding a formula to define experienced truth under pressure of misapprehension and criticism.

The point I shall endeavour to establish is that these statements about God the Creator are not, as is usually supposed, a set of arbitrary mystifications irrelevant to human life and thought. On the contrary, whether or not they are true about God, they are, when examined in the light of direct experience, seen to be plain witness of truth about the nature of the creative mind as such and as we know it. So far as they are applicable to man, they embody a very exact description of the human mind while engaged in an act of creative imagination. Whether this goes to prove that man is made in the image of God, or merely that God has been made in the image of man is an argument that I shall not pursue, since the answer to that question depends upon those historical statements which lie outside my terms of reference. The Christian affirmation is, however, that the Trinitarian structure which can be shown to exist in the mind of man and in all his works is, in fact, the integral structure of the universe, and corresponds, not by pictorial imagery but by a necessary uniformity of substance, with the nature of God, in Whom all that is exists.

MM Preface, pp. ix–x

76

The author on the stage

The whole of existence is held to be the work of the divine Creator – everything that there is, including not only the human maker and his human public, but all other entities 'visible and invisible' that may exist outside this universe. Consequently, whereas the human writer obtains his response from other minds, outside and independent of his own, God's response comes only from His own creatures. This is as though a book were written to be read by the characters within it. And further: the universe is not a finished work. Every mind within it is in the position of the audience sitting in the stalls and seeing the play for the first time. Or rather, every one of us is on the stage, performing a part in a play, of which we have not seen either the script or any synopsis of the ensuing acts.

. . . The actor on the stage of the universe cannot even go to the nearest cinema and see the result of his work when the sequences have been fitted together, for the film is still in the making. At the most, perhaps, towards the end of his life, he may see a few episodes in which he figured run through in the pages of contemporary history. And from the completed episodes of the past he may gather, if he is intelligent and attentive, some indication of the author's purpose.

There is one episode in particular to which Christianity draws his attention. The leading part in this was played, it is alleged, by the Author, who presents it as a brief epitome of the plan of the whole work. If we ask, 'What *kind* of play is this that we are acting?' the answer put forward is: 'Well, it is *this* kind of play.' And examining the plot of it, we observe at once that if anybody in this play has his feelings spared, it is certainly not the Author.

'The Love of the Creature', MM pp. 103–4

77

The image of God

It was said by Kronecker the mathematician: 'God made the integers; all else is the work of man.' Man can table the integers and arrange them into problems which he can solve in the terms in which they are set. But before the inscrutable mystery of the integers themselves he is helpless, unless he calls upon that Tri-Unity in himself which is made in the image of God, and can include and create the integers.

This is the vocation of the creative mind in man. The mind in the act of creation is thus not concerned to solve problems within the limits imposed by the terms in which they are set, but to fashion a synthesis which includes the whole dialectic of the situation in a manifestation of power. In other words, the creative artist, as such, deals, not with the working of the syllogism, but with that universal statement which forms its major premise. That is why he is always a disturbing influence; for all logical argument depends upon acceptance of the major premise, and this, by its nature, is not susceptible of logical proof. The hand of the creative artist, laid upon the major premise, rocks the foundations of the world; and he himself can only indulge in this perilous occupation because his mansion is not in the world but in the eternal heavens.

The artist's knowledge of his own creative nature is often unconscious; he pursues his mysterious way of life in a strange innocence. If he were consciously to pluck out the heart of his mystery, he might say something like this:

I find in myself a certain pattern which I acknowledge as the law of my true nature, and which corresponds to experience in such a manner that, while my behaviour conforms to the pattern, I can interpret experience in power. I find, further, that the same pattern inheres in my work as in myself; and I also find that theologians attribute to God Himself precisely that pattern of being which I find in my work and in me.

I am inclined to believe, therefore, that this pattern directly corresponds to the actual structure of the living universe, and that it exists in other men as well as in myself; and I conclude that, if other men feel themselves to be powerless in the universe and at odds with it, it is because the pattern of their lives and works has become distorted and no longer corresponds to the universal pattern − because they are, in short, running counter to the law of their nature.

I am confirmed in this belief by the fact that, so far as I conform to the pattern of human society, I feel myself also to be powerless and at odds with the universe; while so far as I conform to the pattern of my true nature, I am at odds with human society, and it with me. If I am right in thinking that human society is out of harmony with the law of its proper nature, then my experience again corroborates that of the theologians, who have also perceived this fundamental dislocation in man.

If you ask me what is this pattern which I recognise as the true law of my nature, I can only suggest that it is the pattern of the creative mind – an eternal Idea, manifested in material form by an unresting Energy, with an outpouring of Power that at once inspires, judges, and communicates the work; all these three being one and the same in the mind and one and the same in the work. And this, I observe, is the pattern laid down by the theologians as the pattern of the being of God.

If all this is true, then the mind of the maker and the Mind of the Maker are formed on the same pattern, and all their works are made in their own image.

It is not at all likely that, if you caught the first artist you saw passing and questioned him, he would explain himself in these terms. He is no more accustomed than the rest of us to look for any connection between theology and experience. Nor, as I said at the beginning, do the theologians of to-day take much trouble to expound their doctrine by way of the human maker's analogy. They are ready to use the 'Father-symbol' to illustrate the likeness and familiarity between God and His children. But the 'Creator-symbol' is used, if at all, to illustrate the deep gulf between God and His creatures. Yet, as Berdyaev says, 'The image of the artist and the poet is imprinted more clearly on his works than on his children'. Particularly when it comes to the Trinity of the God-head, the emphasis is always placed on the mystery and unique-ness of the structure – as though it were a kind of blasphemy to recognise with Augustine that this, at least, is to man a homely and intimate thing, 'familiar as his garter'.

The disastrous and widening cleavage between the Church and the Arts on the one hand and between the State and the Arts on the other leaves the common man with the impression that the artist is something of little account, either in this world or the next; and this has had a bad effect on the artist, since it has left him in a curious spiritual isolation. Yet with all his faults, he remains the person who can throw most light on that 'creative attitude to life' to which bewildered leaders of thought are now belatedly exhorting a no less bewildered humanity.

Nor is the creative mind unpractical or aloof from that of the common man. The notion that the artist is a vague, dreamy creature living in retreat from the facts of life is a false one — fostered, as I shrewdly suspect, by those to whose interest it is to keep administrative machinery moving regardless of the end-product. At the irruption of the artist into a State department, officialdom stands aghast, not relishing the ruthless realism which goes directly to essentials. It is for the sacrilegious hand laid on the major premise that the artist is crucified by tyrannies and quietly smothered by bureaucracies. As for the common man, the artist is nearer to him than the man of any other calling, since his vocation is precisely to express the highest common factor of humanity – that image of the Creator which distinguishes the man from the beast. If the common man is to enjoy the divinity of his humanity, he can come to it only in virtue and right of his making.

> The wisdom of a learned man cometh by opportunity of leisure and he that hath little business shall become wise.
>
> How can he get wisdom that holdeth the plough, and that glorieth in the goad, that driveth oxen, and is occupied in their labours, and whose talk is of bullocks?
>
> He giveth his mind to make furrows; and is diligent to give the kine fodder.
>
> So every carpenter and workmaster, that laboureth night and day; and they cut and grave seals, and are diligent to make great variety, and give themselves to counterfeit imagery, and watch to finish a work:
>
> The smith also sitting by the anvil, and considering the iron work, the vapour of the fire wasteth his flesh, and he fighteth with the heat of the furnace: the noise of the hammer and the anvil is ever in his ears, and his eyes look still upon the pattern of the thing that he maketh; he setteth his mind to finish his work, and watcheth to polish it perfectly:
>
> So doth the potter sitting at his work, and turning the

wheel about with his feet, who is alway carefully set at his work, and maketh all his work by number;

He fashioneth the clay with his arm and boweth down its strength before his feet; he applieth himself to lead it over; and he is diligent to make clean the furnace:

All these trust to their hands: and every one is wise in his work.

Without these cannot a city be inhabited: and they shall not dwell where they will, nor go up and down:

They shall not be sought for in public counsel, nor sit high in the congregation: they shall not sit on the judges' seat, nor understand the sentence of judgment; they cannot declare justice and judgment; and they shall not be found where parables are spoken.

But they will maintain the state of the world, and all their desire is in the work of their craft.[1]

'Problem Picture', MM pp. 171–5

A version of Dorothy Sayers' view of the theology of the artist can be found in her essay, 'Towards a Christian Aesthetic' (1944).

[1] Ecclesiasticus xxxviii. 24–34

How do we say that God creates, and how does this compare with the act of creation by an artist? To begin with, of course, we say that God created the universe 'out of nothing' – He was bound by no conditions of any kind. Here there can be no comparison: the human artist is *in* the universe and bound by its conditions. He can create only within that framework and out of that material which the universe supplies. Admitting that, let us ask in what way God creates. Christian theology replies that God, who is a Trinity, creates by, or through, His second Person, His Word or Son, who is continually begotten from the First Person, the Father, in an eternal creative activity. And certain theologians have added this very significant comment: the Father, they say, is only known to Himself by beholding His image in His Son.

Does that sound very mysterious? We will come back to the human artist, and see what it means in terms of *his* activity. But first, let us take note of a new word that has crept into the arguments by way of Christian theology – the word *Image*. Suppose, having rejected the words 'copy', 'imitation' and 'repre-sentation' as inadequate, we substitute the word 'image' and say that what the artist is doing is *to image forth* something or the other, and connect that with St Paul's phrase: 'God . . . hath spoken to us by His Son, the brightness of his glory and *express image* of his person.' – Something which, by being an image, *expresses* that which it images. Is that getting us a little nearer to something? There is something which is, in the deepest sense of the words, *unimaginable*, known to Itself (and still more, to us) only by the image in which it expresses Itself through creation; and, says Christian theology very emphatically, the Son, who is the express image, is not the copy, or imitation, or representation of the Father, nor yet inferior or subsequent to the Father in any way – in the last resort, in the depths of their mysterious being, the Unimaginable and the Image are *one and the same*.

'Towards a Christian Aesthetic', UO pp. 37–8

A poet is a man who not only suffers 'the impact of external events', but experiences them. He puts the experience into words in his own mind, and in so doing recognises the experience for what it is. To the extent that we can do that, we are all poets. A 'poet' so-called is simply a man like ourselves with an exceptional power of revealing his experience by expressing it, so that not only he, but we ourselves, recognise that experience as our own.

I want to stress the word *recognise*. A poet does not see something – say the full moon – and: 'This is a very beautiful sight – let me set about finding words for the appropriate expression of what people ought to feel about it.' That is what the literary artisan does, and it means nothing. What happens is that then, or at some time after, he finds himself saying words in his head and says to himself: 'Yes – that is right. *That* is the experience the full moon was to me. I recognise it in expressing it, and now I know what it was.' And so, when it is a case of mental or spiritual experience – sin, grief, joy, sorrow, worship – the thing reveals itself to him in words, and so becomes fully experienced for the first time. By thus recognising it in its expression, he makes it his own – integrates it into himself. He no longer feels himself battered passively by the impact of external events – it is no longer something happening *to* him, but something happening *in* him, the reality of the event is communicated to him in activity and power. So that the act of the poet in creation is seen to be threefold – a trinity – experience, expression and recognition; the unknowable reality in the experience; the image of that reality known in its expression; and power in the recognition; the whole making up the single and indivisible act of creative mind.

Now, what the poet does for himself, he can also do for us. When he has imaged forth his experience he can incarnate it, so to speak, in a material body – words, music, painting – the thing we know as a work of art. And since he is a man like the rest of us, we shall expect that our experience will have something in common with his. In the image of *his* experience, we can *recognise* the image of some experience of our own – something that had happened to us, but which we had never understood, never formulated or expressed to ourselves, and therefore never known as a real experience. When we read the poem, or see the play or picture or hear the music, it is as though a light were turned on inside us. We say: 'Ah! I recognise that! That is something which I obscurely felt to be going on in and about me, but I didn't know what it was and couldn't express it. But now that the artist has made its image – imaged it forth – for me, I can possess and take hold of it and make it my own, and turn it into a source of knowledge and strength.' This is the *communication of the image in power*, by which the third person of the poet's trinity brings us, through the incarnate image, into direct knowledge of the in itself unknowable and unimaginable reality. 'No man cometh to the Father save by Me,' said the incarnate Image; and He added, 'but the Spirit of Power will lead you into all truth.'

This recognition of the truth that we get in the artist's work comes to us as a revelation of new truth. I want to be clear about that. I am not referring to the sort of patronising recognition we give to a writer by nodding our heads and observing: 'Yes, yes, very good, very true – that's just what I'm always saying.' I mean the recognition of a truth which tells us something about ourselves that we had *not* been 'always saying' – something which puts a new knowledge of ourselves within our grasp. It is new, startling, and perhaps shattering – and yet it comes to us with a sense of familiarity. We did not know it before, but the moment the poet has shown it to us, we know that, somehow or other, we had always really known it.

Very well. But frankly, is that the sort of thing the average British citizen gets, or expects to get, when he goes to the theatre or reads a book? No, it is not. In the majority of cases, it is not in the least what he expects, or what he wants. What he looks for is not this creative and Christian kind of Art at all. He does not expect or desire to be upset by sudden revelations about himself and the universe. Like the people of Plato's decadent Athens, he has forgotten or repudiated the religious origins of all Art. He wants entertainment, or, if he is a little more serious-minded, he wants something with a moral, or to have some spell or incantation put on him to instigate him to virtuous action.

Now, entertainment and moral spell-binding have their uses, but they are not Art in the proper sense. They may be the incidental effects of good art; but they may also be the very aim and essence of false art. And if we continue to demand of the Arts only these two things, we shall starve and silence the true artist and encourage in his place the false artist, who may become a very sinister force indeed.

Let us take the amusement-art: what does that give us? Generally speaking, what we demand and get from it is the enjoyment of the emotions which usually accompany experience without having had the experience. It does not reveal us to ourselves: it merely

84

projects on to a mental screen a picture of ourselves as we already fancy ourselves to be – only bigger and brighter. The manufacturer of this kind of entertainment is not by any means interpreting and revealing his own experience to himself and us – he is either indulging his own day-dreams, or – still more falsely and venially – he is saying: 'What is it the audience think they would like to have experienced? Let us show them that, so that they can wallow in emotion by pretending to have experienced it.' This kind of pseudo-art is 'wish-fulfilment' or 'escape' literature in the worst sense – it is an escape, not from the 'impact of external events' into the citadel of experienced reality, but an escape from reality and experience into a world of merely external events – the progressive externalisation of consciousness. For occasional re-laxation this is all right; but it can be carried to the point where, not merely art, but the whole universe of phenomena becomes a screen on which we see the magnified projection of our unreal selves, as the object of equally unreal emotions. This brings about the complete corruption of the consciousness, which can no longer recognise reality in experience. When things come to this pass, we have a civilisation which 'lives for amusement' – a civilisation without guts, without experience, and out of touch with reality.

Or take the spell-binding kind of art. This at first sight seems better because it spurs us to action; and it also has its uses. But it too is dangerous in excess, because once again it does not reveal reality in experience, but only projects a lying picture of the self. As the amusement-art seeks to produce the *emotions* without the experience, so *this* pseudo-art seeks to produce the *behaviour* without the experience. In the end it is directed to putting the behaviour of the audience beneath the will of the spell-binder, and its true name is not 'art', but 'art-magic.' In its vulgarest form it becomes pure propaganda. It can (as we have reason to know) actually succeed in making its audience into the thing it desires to have them – it can really in the end corrupt the consciousness and destroy experience until the inner selves of its victims are wholly externalised and made the puppets and instruments of their own spurious passions. This is why it is dangerous for anybody – even for the Church – to urge artists to produce works of art for the express purpose of 'doing good to people'. Let her by all means encourage artists to express their own Christian experience and communicate it to others. That is the true artist saying: 'Look!

85

recognise your experience in my own.' But 'edifying art' may only too often be the pseudo-artist corruptly saying: 'This is what you are supposed to believe and feel and do – and I propose to work you into a state of mind in which you will believe and feel and do as you are told.' This pseudo-art does not really communicate power to us; it merely exerts power over us.

What is it, then, that these two pseudo-arts – the entertaining and the spell-binding – have in common? And how are they related to true art? What they have in common is the falsification of the consciousness; and they are to Art as the *idol* is to the Image. The Jews were forbidden to make any image for worship, because before the revelation of the threefold unity in which Image and Unimaginable are one, it was only too fatally easy to substitute the idol for the Image. The Christian revelation set free all the images, by showing that the true Image subsisted within the Godhead Itself – it was neither copy, nor imitation, nor representation, nor inferior, nor subsequent, but the brightness of the glory, and the express image of the Person – the very mirror in which reality knows itself and communicates itself in power.

But the danger still exists; and it always will recur whenever the Christian doctrine of the Image is forgotten. In our æsthetic, that doctrine has never been fully used or understood, and in consequence our whole attitude to the artistic expression of reality has become confused, idolatrous and pagan. We see the Arts degenerating into mere entertainment which corrupts and relaxes our civilisation, and we try in alarm to correct this by demanding a more moralising and bracing kind of Art. But this is only setting up one idol in place of the other. Or we see that Art is becoming idolatrous, and suppose that we can put matters right by getting rid of the representational element in it. But what is wrong is not the representation itself, but the fact that we are looking at, and what we are looking *for*, is not the Image but an idol. Little children, keep yourselves from idols.

It has become a commonplace to say that the Arts are in a bad way. We are in fact largely given over to the entertainers and the spell-binders; and because we do not understand that these two functions do not represent the true nature of Art, the true artists are, as it were, excommunicate, and have no audience. But there is here not, I think, so much a relapse from a Christian æsthetic as a failure ever to find and examine a real Christian æsthetic, based on dogma and not on ethics. This may not be a bad thing. We have at least a new line of country to explore, that has not been trampled on and built over and fought over by countless generations of quarrelsome critics. What we have to start from is the Trinitarian doctrine of creative mind, and the light which that doctrine throws on the true nature of images.

The great thing, I am sure, is not to be nervous about God – not to try and shut out the Lord Immanuel from *any* sphere of truth. Art is not He – we must not substitute Art for God; yet this also is He, for it is one of His Images and therefore reveals His nature. Here we see in a mirror darkly – we behold only the images; elsewhere we shall see face to face, in the place where Image and Reality are one.

'Towards a Christian Aesthetic', UO pp. 39–43

Dorothy Sayers wrote one essay in which she comments briskly not only on Trinitarian theology and its meaning but on belief in the Church, baptism and resurrection, essential to her understanding of the importance of the created world. Before reading the bulk of her 1940 essay 'What do we believe?' it is worth bearing in mind her attempt to explain the importance of Constantine to her public, in a play written for the Colchester Festival of 1951, entitled *The Emperor Constantine: a Chronicle in Three Acts, a Prologue and an Epilogue* covering the years AD 305–326. In the play she puts into context the challenge of Athanasius to those at the Council of Nicea. These two extracts are followed by her own paraphrases of Athanasian orthodoxy.

Who was Constantine, whom Christendom has alternately blessed and cursed? whose ambivalent Church was the double crown of thorns and gold? . . .

His father was Constantine Chlorus, appointed by Diocletian Augustus of the West, to rule the Provinces of Britain, Spain, and Gaul. His mother was that Helena who was later canonised as St Helena, and whose finding of the True Cross in Jerusalem is commemorated in the Church's calendar on the third day of May. It was said by some, both then and now, that she was Constantine's concubine, a woman of humble origin – a barmaid, indeed, from Bithynia. But an ancient and respectable tradition affirms, on the other hand, that she was his lawful wife, a princess of Britain, daughter of the local chieftain 'King' Coel of Colchester, whose legend, distorted by time, is preserved in the nursery song of 'old King Cole'. If this is so – and Colchester will hear no word to the contrary – she may well have been a Christian from her birth; for in the 4th century there was already a Christian church, with a Christian bishop, at Colchester. Her son may thus have received a bias towards Christianity from his early years; his father, Constantius, though not a Christian, was a monotheist and favourably disposed to the Christians, steadily refusing to enforce the edicts of Diocletian against them. Constantine's own story, which he told to his biographer, Eusebius of Caesarea, is this. He said that one day, as he was riding across a plain in Gaul during his campaign against Maxentius, he saw a strange appearance round about the sun – the sign of the Chi-Ro, written in fire upon the sky; and that on the following night, in his tent, One came and showed him the sign again, saying to him: '*Hoc signo victor eris*: with this sign thou shalt be victor.' And learning that the Chi and the Ro were the first letters of the name of Christ, he set the sign upon his shields, and the victory followed.

Thenceforth he was the elect servant of Christ. Yet we know that even before that time he was not indifferent to Christianity, for already among his most intimate counsellors he counted a Christian Bishop, the venerable Hosius of Cordova.

It seems possible to trace, running through the recorded acts, words, and writings of Constantine, a consistently developing apprehension of Christ. There is the Christ known to the pagan world, one god among many, worshipped by an increasingly numerous sect whose sober and disciplined life made it a valuable element in the State; there is Christ the Lord of Hosts, the powerful patron-deity of His Imperial Vicar; there is, later on, the Christ of the theologians, True God begotten of True God, the Holy and the One; there is, perhaps, in the end of all, Christ the Redeemer, sacrificed upon the wood of the Cross for the sins of man – and of Constantine.

EC, Preface pp. 7–8

Athanasius at the Council of Nicea, AD 325

. . . Beloved Fathers, in whom will you believe? In the Christ of Arius, who is neither true Man to bear our sorrows nor true God to forgive us our sins? Or in Him who, being in the form of God, clung not to His equality with God, but was made in the likeness of man and became obedient unto death for our sakes? Reasoning is but words – God's act is the living truth. I call upon the martyrs to say for whom they suffered.

EC Act 3 Scene 5, p. 149

'We believe in One God, the Father Almighty, Maker of all things visible and invisible. And in One Lord Jesus Christ, the Son of God, sole-begotten of the Father's substance, God out of God, Light out of Light, True God out of True God, begotten not made, consubstantial with the Father. By Whom also all things were made, both things in Heaven and things in earth. Who for us men and our salvation came down and was made flesh, lived among men as man, suffered, and rose again the third day, ascended into Heaven, and cometh to judge the quick and the dead.

And we believe in the Holy Ghost.'

EC Act 3 Scene 5, p. 159

What do we believe?

I believe in God the Father Almighty, Maker of all things. That is the thundering assertion with which we start: that the great fundamental quality that makes God, and us with Him, what we are is creative activity. After this, we can scarcely pretend that there is anything negative, static, or sedative about the Christian religion. 'In the beginning God created'; from everlasting to everlasting, He is God the Father and Maker. And, by implication, man is most godlike and most himself when he is occupied in creation. And by this statement we assert further that the will and power to make is an absolute value, the ultimate good-in-itself, self-justified, and self-explanatory.

How far can we check this assertion as it concerns ourselves? The men who create with their minds and those who create (not merely labour) with their hands will, I think, agree that their periods of creative activity are those in which they feel right with themselves and the world. And those who bring life into the world will tell you the same thing. There is a psychological theory that artistic creation is merely a 'compensation' for the frustration of sexual creativeness; but it is more probable that the making of life is only one manifestation of the universal urge to create. Our worst trouble to-day is our feeble hold on creation. To sit down and let ourselves be spoon-fed with the ready-made is to lose grip on our only true life and our only real selves.

And in the only-begotten Son of God, by whom all things were made. He was incarnate; crucified, dead and buried; and rose again. The second statement warns us what to expect when the creative energy is manifested in a world subject to the forces of destruction. It makes things and manifests Itself in time and matter, and can no other, because It is begotten of the creative will. So doing, It suffers through the opposition of other wills, as well as through the dead resistance of inertia. (There is no room here to discuss whether will is 'really' free; if we did not, in fact, *believe* it to be free, we could neither act nor live.)

The creative will presses on to Its end, regardless of what It may suffer by the way. It does not choose suffering, but It will not avoid it, and must expect it. We say that It is Love, and 'sacrifices' Itself for what It loves; and this is true, provided we understand what we mean by sacrifice. Sacrifice is what it looks like to other people, but to That-which-Loves I think it does not appear so. When one really cares, the self is forgotten, and the sacrifice becomes only a part of the activity. Ask yourself: If there is something you supremely want to do, do you count as 'self-sacrifice' the difficulties encountered or the other possible activities cast aside? You do not. The time when you deliberately say, 'I must sacrifice this, that, or the other' is when you do not *supremely* desire the end in view. At such times you are doing your duty, and that is admirable, but it is not love. But as soon as your duty becomes your love the 'self-sacrifice' is taken for granted, and, whatever the world calls it, you call it so no longer.

Moreover, defeat cannot hold the creative will; it can pass through the grave and rise again. If It cannot go by the path of co-operation, It will go by the path of death and victory. But it does us no credit if we force It to go that way. It is our business to recognise It when It appears and lead It into the city with hosannas. If we betray It or do nothing to assist It, we may earn the unenviable distinction of going down in history with Judas and Pontius Pilate.

I believe in the Holy Ghost, the lord and life-giver. In this odd and difficult phrase the Christian affirms that the life in him proceeds from the eternal creativeness; and that therefore so far as he is moved by that creativeness, and so far only, he is truly alive. The word 'ghost' is difficult to us; the alternative word 'spirit' is in some ways more difficult still, for it carries with it still more complicated mental associations. The Greek word is *pneuma*, breath: 'I believe in the breath of life.' And indeed, when we are asked, 'What do you value more than life?' the answer can only be, 'Life – the right kind of life, the creative and godlike life'. And life, of any kind, can only be had if we are ready to lose life altogether – a plain observation of fact which we acknowledge every time a child is born, or, indeed, whenever we plunge into a stream of traffic in the hope of attaining a more desirable life on the other side.

And I believe in one Church and baptism, in the resurrection of the body and the life everlasting. The final clauses define what Christians believe about man and matter. First, that all those who believe in the creative life are members of one another and make up the present body in which that life is manifest. They accept for themselves everything that was affirmed of creative life incarnate, including the love and, if necessary, the crucifixion, death and victory. Looking at what happened to that Life, they will expect to be saved, not *from* danger and suffering, but *in* danger and suffering. And the resurrection of the body means more, I think, than we are accustomed to suppose. It means that, whatever happens, there can be no end to the manifestation of creative life. Whether the life makes its old body again, or an improved body, or a totally new body, it will and must create, since that is its true nature.

'This is the Christian faith, which except a man believe faithfully he cannot be saved.' The harsh and much-disputed statement begins to look like a blunt statement of fact; for how can anyone make anything of his life if he does not believe in life? If we truly desire a creative life for ourselves and other people, it is our task to rebuild the world along creative lines; but we must be sure that we desire it enough.

'What do we believe?', UO pp. 18–20

And here is one further example. To appreciate particular emphases in her reading of Dante (first mediated in *The Just Vengeance* written for Lichfield Cathedral in 1946), and her attention to the resurrection narratives of the gospels in her brilliantly successful radio plays, *The Man Born to be King* (1941–2), consider this evaluation of the material world in its relation to God:

If ... the Church, as a Christian society, is concerned with civilization, or with politics and economics, it can only be on the grounds of a realistic and sacramental theology of the Incarnation. For this means that the whole of man's humanity, at its most vital, developed, and characteristic, is the vehicle of the divine part of his nature; that he cannot grow nearer to God by dissociating himself from his own humanity, or from the rest of humanity; but that, on the contrary, the response of the Spirit to the Father is best expressed in the response of a fully developed and characteristically human society.

This, indeed, both Bethlehem and Pentecost would lead us to expect. But we must add this rider: that a Church which takes up this fully sacramental position must not confine her concern with civilization to the political and economic aspects of civilization. If she undertakes to sanctify humanity, it must be the *whole* of humanity. She must include within her sacraments all arts, all letters, all labour and all learning; she must not put a premium upon stupidity, nor must she confine her interest in the witness of man's body to precautionary measures of sanitation, and the regulation of appetite under the Law. For she stands committed to the assertion that all human activity, whether of spirit, mind or body, is potentially good – not negatively, by repression, but positively, and as an act of worship. Further, she must include a proper reverence for the earth and for all material things; because these also are the body of the living God.

ML pp. 66–7

95

6

THE MAN
BORN TO BE KING

=

Dorothy Sayers' radio play, *He That Should Come*, of
Christmas Day 1938, was some sort of preparation for the
much more ambitious venture of writing twelve radio plays
(the first broadcast of which began on 21 December 1941)
under the title, *The Man Born to be King*. We have in our
day almost lost the sense of scandal provoked in some of her
detractors by those radio plays in their time. Some Christians
gave her excellent publicity *gratis*, partly out of a mixture
of panic and ignorance sometimes characteristic of the sup-
posedly devout, and partly because of the sheer unfamiliarity
of hearing the 'voice' of Jesus of Nazareth. She was of course
quite inadvertently helping to open the doors to all sorts of
versions of the Gospel on stage and screen, and it is not too
difficult to guess what she would have thought of some of
these productions, sentimental rather than sacramental por-
trayals of Christ, and lacking in intellectual stringency as well
as human vitality. The introductory poem on 'The Makers'
recalls *Zeal* as well as her concentration on an understanding
of human in relation to divine creativity. The next extract re-
emphasizes and elaborates her 'Note to Producers' for *He
That Should Come* but with a clearly apologetic focus on her
critics. The third is an extract from the Epiphany to the Kings
in the shepherd's cottage from the very first play, *Kings in
Judaea*.

The Makers

The Architect stood forth and said:
  'I am the master of the art:
I have the thought within my head,
  I have a dream within my heart.

'Come now, good craftsman, ply your trade
  With tool and stone obediently;
Behold the plan that I have made —
  I am the master; serve you me.'

The Craftsman answered: 'Sir, I will
  Yet look to it that this your draft
Be of a sort to serve my skill —
  You are not master of the craft.

'It is by me the towers grow tall,
  I lay the course, I shape and hew;
You make a little inky scrawl,
  And that is all that you can do.

'Account me then, the master man,
  Laying my rigid rule upon
The plan, and that which serves the plan —
  The uncomplaining, helpless stone.'

The Stone made answer: 'Masters mine,
  Know this: that I can bless or damn
The thing that both of you design
  By being but the thing I am;

'For I am granite and not gold,
  For I am marble and not clay,
You may not hammer me nor mould —
  I am the master of the way.

'Yet once that mastery bestowed
  Then I will suffer patiently
The cleaving steel, the crushing load,
  That make a calvary of me:

97

'And you may carve me with your hand
    To arch and buttress, roof and wall,
Until the dream rise up and stand –
    Serve but the stone, the stone serves all.

'Let each do well what each knows best,
    Nothing refuse and nothing shirk,
Since none is master of the rest,
    But all are servants of the work –

'The work no master may subject
    Save He to whom the whole is known,
Being Himself the Architect,
    The Craftsman and the Corner-stone.

'Then, when the greatest and the least
    Have finished all their labouring
And sit together at the feast,
    You shall behold a wonder thing:

'The Maker of the men that make
    Will stoop between the cherubim,
The towel and the basin take,
    And serve the servants who serve Him.'

The Architect and Craftsman both
    Agreed, the Stone had spoken well;
Bound them to service by an oath
    And each to his own labour fell.

MBK pp. 7–8

On writing *The Man Born to be King*

... My object was *to tell that story* to the best of my ability, within the medium at my disposal – in short, to make as good a work of art as I could. For a work of art that is not good and true *in art* is not true in any other respect, and is useless for any purpose whatsoever – even for edification – because it is a lie, and the devil is the father of all such. As drama, these plays stand or fall. The idea that religious plays are not to be judged by the proper standard of drama derives from a narrow and lop-sided theology which will not allow truth – including the artist's truth – is in Christ, but persists in excluding the Lord of Truth from His own dominions.

What this actually means is that the theology – the dogma – must be taken by the writer as part of the material with which he works, and not as an exterior end towards which his work is directed. Dogma is the grammar and vocabulary of his art. ...

... Accordingly, it is the business of the dramatist not to subordinate the drama to the theology, but to approach the job of truth-telling from his own end, and trust the theology to emerge undistorted from the dramatic presentation of the story. This it can scarcely help doing, if the playwright is faithful to his material, since the history and the theology of Christ are one thing: His life is theology in action, and the drama of His life is dogma shown as dramatic action.

For Jesus Christ is unique – unique among gods and men. There have been incarnate gods a-plenty, and slain-and-resurrected gods not a few; but He is the only God who has a date in history. And plenty of founders of religions have had dates, and some of them have been prophets or avatars of the Divine; but only this one of them was personally God. There is no more astonishing collocation of phrases than that which, in the Nicene Creed, sets these two statements flatly side by side: 'Very God of very God . . . He suffered under Pontius Pilate.' All over the world, thousands of times a day, Christians recite the name of a rather undistinguished Roman pro-consul – not in execration (Judas and Caiaphas, more guilty, get off with fewer reminders of their iniquities), but merely because that name fixes within a few years the date of the death of God.

In the light of that remarkable piece of chronology we can see an additional reason why the writer of realistic Gospel plays has to eschew the didactic approach to his subject. He has to display the words and actions of actual people engaged in living through a piece of recorded history. He cannot, like the writer of purely liturgical or symbolic religious drama, confine himself to the abstract and universal aspect of the life of Christ. He is brought up face to face with the 'scandal of particularity'. *Ecce homo* – not only Man-in-general and God-in-His-thusness, but also God-in-His-thisness, and *this* Man, *this* person, of a reasonable soul and human flesh subsisting, who walked and talked *then* and *there*, surrounded, not by human types, but by *those* individual people. This story of the life and murder and resurrection of God-in-Man is not only the symbol and epitome of the relations of God and man throughout time; it is also a series of events that took place at a particular point *in* time. *And the people of that time had not the faintest idea that it was happening.*

Of all examples of the classical tragic irony in fact or fiction, this is the greatest – the classic of classics. Beside it, the doom of Oedipus is trifling, and the nemesis of the Oresteian blood-bath a mere domestic incident. For the Christian affirmation is that a number of quite commonplace human beings, in an obscure province of the Roman Empire, killed and murdered God Almighty – quite casually, almost as a matter of religious and political routine, and certainly with no notion that they were doing anything out of the way. Their motives, on the whole, were defensible, and in some respects praiseworthy. There was some malice, some weakness, and no doubt some wresting of the law – but no more than we are accustomed to find in the conduct of human affairs. By no juggling of fate, by no unforeseeable coincidence, by no supernatural machinations, but by that destiny which is character, and by the unimaginative following of their ordinary standards of behaviour, they were led, with a ghastly inevitability, to the commission of the crime of crimes. We, the audience, know what they were doing; the whole point and poignancy of the tragedy is lost unless we realise that they did not. It is in this knowledge by the audience of the appalling truth which is hidden from all the agonists in the drama that the tragic irony consists.

MBK Introduction, pp. 20–1

To make an *adequate* presentation of the life of God Incarnate would require literally superhuman genius, in playwright and actors alike. We are none of us, I think, under any illusions about our ability to do what the greatest artists who ever lived would admit to be beyond their powers. Nevertheless, when a story is great enough, any honest craftsman may succeed in producing something not altogether unworthy, because the greatness is in the story, and does not need to borrow anything from the craftsman; it is enough that he should faithfully serve the work.

But the craftsman must be honest, and must know what work he is serving. I am a writer and I know my trade; and I say that this story is a very great story indeed, and deserves to be taken seriously. I say further (and here I know what I am saying and mean exactly what I say) that in these days it is seldom taken seriously. It is often taken, and treated, with a gingerly solemnity: but that is what honest writers call frivolous treatment.

Not Herod, not Caiaphas, not Pilate, not Judas ever contrived to fasten upon Jesus Christ the reproach of insipidity; that final indignity was left for pious hands to inflict. To make of His story something that could neither startle, nor shock, nor terrify, not excite, nor inspire a living soul is to crucify the Son of God afresh and put Him to an open shame. And if anybody imagines that its conventional presentation has of late been all that it should be, let him stop the next stranger in the street and ask what effect it has had on *him*. Or let him look at the world to which this Gospel has been preached for close on twenty centuries: *Si calvarium, si sepulchrum requiris, circumspice*. Let me tell you, good Christian people, an honest writer would be ashamed to treat a nursery tale as you have treated the greatest drama in history: and this in virtue, not of his faith, but of his calling.

You have forgotten, perhaps, that it is, first and foremost, a story – a true story, the turning-point of history, 'the only thing that has ever really happened'. If so, the humblest in our kind may venture to put you in mind of it – we the playwright and the players – because it is our craft to tell stories, and that is the only craft we know. We have done what we could; may the Master Craftsman amend all.

MBK Introduction, pp. 36–7

101

Manifestation

CASPAR: O lady clear as the sun, fair as the moon, the nations of the earth salute your son, the Man born to be King. Hail, Jesus, King of the Jews!

MELCHIOR: Hail, Jesus, King of the World!

BALTHAZAR: Hail, Jesus, King of Heaven!

CASPAR:
MELCHIOR: } All Hail!
BALTHAZAR:

MARY: God bless you, wise old man; and you, tall warrior; and you, dark traveller from desert lands. You come in a strange way, and with a strange message. But that God sent you I am sure, for you and His angels speak with one voice. 'King of the Jews' – why, yes; they told me my son should be the Messiah of Israel. 'King of the World' – that is a very great title; yet when he was born, they proclaimed tidings of joy to all nations. 'King of Heaven' – I don't quite understand that; and yet indeed they said that he should be called the Son of God. You are great and learned men, and I am a very simple woman. What can I say to you, till the time comes when my son can answer for himself?

CASPAR: Alas! the more we know, the less we understand life. Doubts make us afraid to act, and much learning dries the heart. And the riddle that torments the world is this: Shall Wisdom and Love live together at last, when the promised Kingdom comes?

MELCHIOR: We are rulers, and we see that what men need most is good government, with freedom and order. But order puts fetters on freedom, and freedom rebels against order, so that love and power are always at war together. And the riddle that torments the world is this: Shall Power and Love dwell together at last, when the promised Kingdom comes?

BALTHAZAR: I speak for a sorrowful people – for the ignorant and the poor. We rise up to labour and lie down to sleep, and night is only a pause between one burden and another. Fear is our daily companion – the fear of want, the fear of war, the fear of cruel death, and of still more cruel life. But all this we could bear if we knew that we did not suffer in vain; that God was beside us in the struggle, sharing the miseries of His own world. For the riddle that torments the world is this: Shall Sorrow and Love be reconciled at last, when the promised Kingdom comes?

MARY: These are very difficult questions – but with me, you see, it is like this. When the Angel's message came to me, the Lord put a song into my heart. I suddenly saw that wealth and cleverness were nothing to God – no one is too unimportant to be His friend. That was the thought that came to me, because of the thing that happened to *me*. I am quite humbly born, yet the Power of God came upon me; very foolish and unlearned, yet the Word of God was spoken to me; and I was in deep distress, when my Baby was born and filled my life with love. So I know very well that Wisdom and Power and Sorrow *can* live together with Love; and for me, the Child in my arms is the answer to all the riddles.

CASPAR: You have spoken a wise word, Mary. Blessed are you among women, and blessed is Jesus your son. Caspar, King of Chaldaea, salutes the King of the Jews with a gift of frankincense.

MELCHIOR: O Mary, you have spoken a word of power. Blessed are you among women, and blessed is Jesus your son. Melchior, King of Pamphylia, salutes the King of the World with a gift of gold.

BALTHAZAR: You have spoken a loving word, Mary, Mother of God. Blessed are you among women, and blessed is Jesus your son. Balthazar, King of Ethiopia, salutes the King of Heaven with a gift of myrrh and spices.

MBK Kings in Judaea, Scene II, pp. 58–9

The next extract also comes from her 'Introduction' and explains her own remarkable creation of Judas' character, following on from her exploration of pride in Faustus and William. The other extracts are short passages from a variety of scenes, culminating in the resurrection scenes.

After Faustus and William, Judas

Judas in the Gospels is an enigma. He is introduced suddenly, at a late moment in the action, 'all set' for villainy. We are not told how he came to be a disciple, nor what motives drove him to betray his Master. St John says he was a thief; he certainly took payment for his treason; Jesus called him *'diabolos'* – the enemy – and 'the son of perdition'; when he had done his worst and saw what he had done, he brought back the reward of iniquity and went out and hanged himself. He seems a strange mixture of the sensitive and the insensitive. One thing is certain: he cannot have been the creeping, drawling, patently worthless villain that some simple-minded people would like to make out; that would be to cast too grave a slur upon the brains or the character of Jesus. To choose an obvious crook as one's follower, in ignorance of what he was like, would be the act of a fool; and Jesus of Nazareth was no fool, and indeed St John expressly says that 'He knew what was in' Judas from the beginning. But to choose an obvious crook for the express purpose of letting him damn himself would be the act of a devil; for a man, *a fortiori* for a God, who behaved like that, nobody – except perhaps Machiavelli – could feel any kind of respect. But also (and this is far more important for our purpose), either of these sorts of behaviour would be totally irreconcilable with the rest of the character of Jesus as recorded. You might write an anti-Christian tract making Him out to be weak-minded and stupid; you might even write a theological treatise of the pre-destinarian sort making Him out to be beyond morality; but there is no means whatever by which you could combine either of these theories with the rest of His words and deeds *and make a play of them.* The glaring inconsistencies in the character would wreck the show: no honest dramatist could write such a part; no actor could play it; no intelligent audience could accept it. That is what I mean by saying that dramatic handling is a stern test of theology, and that the dramatist must tackle the material from his own end of the job. No; the obviously villainous Judas will not do, either dramatically or theologically – the most damnable of all sins is a subtler thing than any crude ambition or avarice. The worst evil in the world is brought about, not by the open and self-confessed vices, but by the deadly corruption of the proud virtues. Pride, which cast Lucifer the Archangel out of

Heaven and Adam out of the Eden of primal innocence, is the head and front of all sin, and the besetting sin of highly virtuous and intelligent people. Jesus, who dealt gently with 'publicans and sinners', was hard as nails about the lofty-minded sins; He was a consistent person, and if He spoke of Judas with almost unexampled sternness, it is likely that the sin of Judas was of a peculiarly overweening loftiness. What his familiar devil precisely was, we are at liberty to conjecture; I have conjectured that it was an intellectual devil of a very insidious kind, very active in these days and remarkably skilful in disguising itself as an angel of light. The fact that various persons have written angrily to say that the Judas I have depicted seems to them to be a person of the utmost nobility, actuated by extremely worthy motives, confirms my impression that this particular agent of hell is at present doing his master's work with singular thoroughness and success. His exploits go unrecognised – which is just what the devil likes best.

MBK Introduction, pp. 30–1

A disciple's experience

MATTHEW: Ah! makes you feel bad, he does, sometimes. Laughs and talks and eats with you – and all the time you know you're not fit to touch him. . . . I shan't forget my first sight of him neither. You don't know me, mister – well, I'll tell you, I was a tax-gatherer. You know what to think about that: I can see it in your face. One of the dirty dogs that works for the government and makes his profit out of selling his countrymen. That's so, and you're dead right. . . . Well, see here. When he came down our street the other day, I don't mind telling you I'd had a pretty good morning. Patting myself on the back, I was, thinking how I'd managed to put the screw on some of those poor devils of farmers and salt away a tidy bit for a rainy day. 'Matthew,' I said to myself, 'you're getting a warm man.' And I looked up – and there he was. 'Hullo!' I thought, 'here's the Prophet. I suppose he'll start calling me names like the rest of 'em. Let him. Hard words break no bones.' So I stared at him, and he stared at me – seemed as though his eyes were going straight through me and through me ledgers, and reading all the bits as wasn't for publication. And somehow or other he made me feel dirty. That's all. Just dirty. I started shuffling my feet. And he smiled – you know the way he smiles sometimes all of a sudden – and he says, 'Follow me'. I couldn't believe my ears. I tumbled out of my desk, and away he went up the street, and I went after him. I could hear people laughing – somebody spat at me – but I didn't seem to care.

MBK *The Heirs to the Kingdom* Scene I, p. 121

Jesus teaches

JESUS: Never think that I have come to destroy the Law. I am here to show you how to keep it. For the old Law says: 'Thou shalt do no murder', and lays down how murderers are to be punished. But *I* say: 'Never hate anybody – for hatred is what leads to murder – it *is* murder; when you hate your fellow-man there is murder in your heart. And the old Law said: 'If you take an oath, you must keep it.' But *I* say, 'Think truth and speak truth, and then there will be no need to insult God with oaths.' And the old Law said: 'Revenge must be kept within limits: an eye for an eye, a tooth for a tooth and no more.' But *I* say, 'Take no revenge at all. If a man hits you once, let him hit you again if he feels like it; if he is mean to you, take pains to be generous to him; if he makes demands upon you, give him double what he asks, and so coax out the bitterness from his heart.' And the old Law said: 'Love your friends and hate your enemies.' But *I* say: 'Anybody can do that. Give up this bargaining attitude altogether. Love even your enemies, do them all the good you can, and when they treat you badly, pray for them. Be like your Father in Heaven, who sends His rain to water the earth for all men, good and evil alike.' Behave to every man as you would like him to behave to you – for this is the way to keep the Law and fulfil all the teaching of the prophets.

MBK *The Heirs to the Kingdom* Scene III, p. 129

On the road to Jerusalem: staying with friends

JOHN: ... It's lovely and cool out here. I think sunset is the pleasantest hour of the day.

MARY: And autumn is the pleasantest season. Look at the leaves of the vine – so green with the light slanting through them – and the dappled shadows dancing on the pavement.

LAZARUS: The leaves will not be green much longer. They are beginning to fall already.

MARY: They are beautiful when they fall – red and yellow and russet-brown, crisped and curled at the edges. When the wind blows them along the ground they make a little whispering noise as though they were telling a gay secret. . . . But Lazarus is always sad in the autumn. Rabbi, tell my brother he should be merrier.

LAZARUS: In a world like this, what is there to be merry about? There is much labour and great disquiet, fear, and a little trembling laughter. The most a man can hope for is tranquillity, and perhaps even that is too much to expect. I think there is a terror at the heart of God's mystery. Is it not so, Rabbi? Is not the fear of the Lord the beginning of wisdom?

JESUS (*dreamily*): 'When He established the foundations of the earth, I was with Him forming all things, and I was delighted every day, playing before Him, playing in the world and delighting myself among the sons of men.'

JOHN (*a little startled – it sounds almost autobiographical*): Master, of whom is that said?

JESUS: Of the Word and Wisdom of God.

LAZARUS: Does joy go so deep as that? To the very foundations of the world? . . .

MBK *The Light and the Life* Scene I, pp. 186–7

108

We have no need of words, my son and I

MARY VIRGIN: My child. When he was small, I washed and fed him; I dressed him in his little garments and combed the rings of his hair. When he cried, I comforted him; when he was hurt, I kissed away the pain; and when the darkness fell, I sang him to sleep. Now he goes faint and fasting in the dust, and his hair is tangled with thorns. They will strip him naked to the sun and hammer the nails into his living flesh, and the great darkness will cover him. And there is nothing I can do. Nothing at all. This is the worst thing; to conceive beauty in your heart and bring it forth into the world, and then to stand by helpless and watch it suffer. . . .

MARY MAGDALEN: How can you speak so calmly?

MARY VIRGIN: While we await the stroke, our minds are confused, wondering how it will come. But when once it has fallen, we are quiet, because there is nothing left to look for. Then everything becomes suddenly very clear – each fact distinct and lucid with its truth. . . . I know now what he is, and what I am. . . . I, Mary, am the fact; God is the truth; but Jesus is fact and truth – he is reality. You cannot see the immortal truth till it is born in the flesh of the fact. And because all birth is a sundering of the flesh, fact and reality seem to go separate ways. But it is not really so; the feet that must walk this road were made of me. Only one Jesus is to die today – one person whom you know – the truth of God and the fact of Mary. This is reality. From the beginning of time until now, this is the only thing that has ever really happened. When you understand this you will understand all prophecies, and all history . . .

MBK *King of Sorrows* Scene I, pp. 294–5

109

Some time later – 1

JOHN (*he is out of breath*): Peter! Peter! It's true. . . . I got there and looked in. . . . There's nobody there. . . . Nothing. . . . Only the linen clothes lying on the grave-slab.

PETER: Where are the women?

JOHN: Heaven knows! – gone out by the other gate, perhaps. . . . Come and look, Peter. . . . Look there! . . . the Lord's body is gone.

PETER: Who can have taken it?

JOHN: *Did anybody take it?*

PETER: What's that you say?

JOHN: I don't know what I'm saying.

PETER: I'm going in to see.

JOHN (*whispering to himself*): Oh, Master, Master – is it possible? . . . this is the third day. . . . No! I daren't say it. . . . I daren't think it. . . .

PETER: John! . . . there's something queer about this. . . . The grave-clothes are here. *The grave-clothes.* . . . What sort of robbers steal the body and leave the grave-clothes behind?

JOHN: Let me come.

PETER: See there, where the body lay. . . . The grave-bands, criss-crossed and wound together from breast to foot . . . and the napkin – not tossed with the rest, but wrapped up by itself – just where his head must have been. . . . Who can have arranged them like that – and in Heaven's name, why?

JOHN: Nobody? – nobody! . . . Can't you see? – They have never been unwound. . . . Look! here is a bundle of myrrh still fast among the folds.

PETER: Never unwound? – You are mad! How could the body have passed —— ?

JOHN: Risen and gone? Risen and gone! – O Jesus! my friend and my living Lord!

MBK *The King Comes into His Own* Scene I, pp. 329–30

Some time later – 2

EVANGELIST: Then the disciples went away again into their own home. But Mary Magdalen returned to the sepulchre and stood without, weeping. And as she wept, she stooped down, and seeth two angels in white sitting, one at the head, and the other at the foot, where the body of Jesus had lain.

RAPHAEL: Gabriel, messenger of the Most High, is our joyful errand done?

GABRIEL: Nearly done, Raphael, son of consolation.

RAPHAEL: Did those women understand us? They were very much afraid.

GABRIEL: They understood more than the soldiers. And in time, they will understand everything.

RAPHAEL: Those disciples did not see us at all.

GABRIEL: John son of Zebedee needs no angel. For his heart is close to the life of the Blessed ――

RAPHAEL: To whom be glory ――

GABRIEL: And dominion for ever ――

RAPHAEL: Amen.

GABRIEL: And the eyes of Peter are darkened with sin and shame. But to him the All-Beautiful will speak ――

RAPHAEL: Whose delight is in mercy ――

GABRIEL: Amen.

RAPHAEL: But what of this woman, who stands and weeps without?

GABRIEL: We will show ourselves to her. Yet she will not heed us. For her love still clings to the mortal flesh she knew. . . . Woman, why do you weep?

MARY MAGDALEN: Because they have taken away my Lord, and I don't know where they have laid him.

(She turns away sobbing)

RAPHAEL: She has turned away.

GABRIEL: Say nothing. He is coming, before whose feet the wilderness breaks into blossom ――

THE ANGELS *(together softly)*: Eloi, Eloi, Eloi. . . .

(MARY MAGDALEN continues to weep)

JESUS: My girl, what are you crying for?

MARY MAGDALEN: Oh, Sir! What has become of him? . . . Are you the gardener? I beg you, if you have hidden him – if he

111

must not lie here in your garden – tell me where you have put him and I will come and take him away. . . . Please – please – I beseech you ——

JESUS: Mary!

MARY MAGDALEN (*with a wild cry*): Rabboni!

JESUS: Do not hold me – do not cling to me now. Not yet. I have not yet gone to the Father. Till then you cannot possess me wholly. . . . Go now, run to my brothers and say to them: I am going home to my Father and to your Father, and my God and your God.

THE EVANGELIST: Then Mary Magdalen came and told the disciples that she had seen the Lord. But the words seemed to them as idle tales, and they believed them not.

MBK The King Comes into His Own Scene I, pp. 330–1

THOMAS: You can all say what you like. Seeing's believing. I tell you again – unless I see in his hands the print of the nails – no, seeing's not enough! Until I have felt with my finger the print of the nails – until I grasp and hold him and thrust my hand into his side, I'll believe nothing.

MATTHEW: Reely, Thomas! Anyody'd think you didn't *want* it to be true.

THOMAS: Wishful thinking won't do. I want proof. And when I say proof ——

JOHN: Hush, Thomas. He's here.

JESUS: Peace be unto you.

DISCIPLES: And to you.

JESUS: Come here, Thomas. Put out your finger and feel my hands. Reach out your hand and thrust it into my side. And doubt no longer, but believe.

THOMAS (*with absolute conviction*): You are my Lord and my God.

(*The crucial word is spoken at last, and received in complete silence*)

JESUS: Thomas, because you have seen me, you have believed. Blessed are they that have not seen, and yet have believed.

PETER (*who has suddenly become aware of some appalling implications*): Master – when I disowned you – when we disbelieved and doubted you – when we failed and deserted and betrayed you – is that what we do to God?

JESUS: Yes, Peter.

JAMES: Lord, when they mocked and insulted and spat upon you – when they flogged you – when they howled for your blood – when they nailed you to the cross and killed you – is that what we do to God?

JESUS: Yes, James.

JOHN: Beloved, when you patiently suffered all things, and went down to death with all our sins heaped upon you – is that what God does for us?

JESUS: Yes, John. For you, and with you, and in you, when you are freely mine. For you are not slaves, but sons. Free to be false or faithful, free to reject or confess me, free to crucify

113

God or be crucified with Him, sharing the shame and sorrow, and the bitter cross and the glory. They that die with me rise with me also, being one with me, as I and my Father are one.

JOHN: This, then, is the meaning of the age-old sacrifice – the blood of the innocent for the sins of the world.

JESUS: Draw near. Receive the breath of God. As the Father sent me forth, so I send you. The guilt that you absolve shall be absolved, and the guilt that you condemn shall be condemned. And peace be upon you.

MBK *The King Comes into His Own* Scene II, pp. 339–40

Dorothy Sayers' 1938 essay, 'The Greatest Drama Ever Staged', which is a short summary of her Christology, provides here a concluding piece from that phase of her writing concerned directly with the Gospels as she read them in the light of the Church's creeds and traditions. Following it is a short reflection from a companion piece, 'The Triumph of Easter'.

The Greatest Drama Ever Staged

Official Christianity, of late years, has been having what is known as 'a bad press'. We are constantly assured that the churches are empty because preachers insist too much upon doctrine – 'dull dogma', as people call it. The fact is the precise opposite. It is the neglect of dogma that makes for dullness. The Christian faith is the most exciting drama that ever staggered the imagination of man – and the dogma *is* the drama.

That drama is summarised quite clearly in the creeds of the Church, and if we think it dull it is because we either have never really read those amazing documents, or have recited them so often and so mechanically as to have lost all sense of their meaning. The plot pivots upon a single character, and the whole action is the answer to a single central problem: *What think ye of Christ?* Before we adopt any of the unofficial solutions (some of which are indeed excessively dull) – before we dismiss Christ as a myth, an idealist, a demagogue, a liar or a lunatic – it will do no harm to find out what the creeds really say about Him. What does the Church think of Christ?

The Church's answer is categorical and uncompromising, and it is this: That Jesus Bar-Joseph, the carpenter of Nazareth, was in fact and in truth, and in the most exact and literal sense of the words, the God 'by Whom all things were made'. His body and brain were those of a common man; His personality was the personality of God, so far as that personality could be expressed in human terms. He was not a kind of dæmon or fairy pretending to be human; He was in every respect a genuine living man. He was not merely a man so good as to be 'like God' – He *was* God.

Now, this is not just a pious commonplace; it is not commonplace at all. For what it means is this, among other things: that for whatever reason God chose to make man as he is – limited and suffering and subject to sorrows and death – He had the honesty and the courage to take His own medicine. Whatever game He is playing with His creation, He has kept His own rules and played fair. He can exact nothing from man that He has not exacted from Himself. He has Himself gone through the whole of human experience, from the trivial irritations of family life and the cramping restrictions of hard work and lack of money to the worst horrors of pain and humiliation, defeat, despair and death.

When He was a man, He played the man. He was born in poverty and died in disgrace and thought it well worth while.

Christianity is, of course, not the only religion that has found the best explanation of human life in the idea of an incarnate and suffering god. The Egyptian Osiris died and rose again; Æschylus in his play, *The Eumenides*, reconciled man to God by the theory of a suffering Zeus. But in most theologies, the god is supposed to have suffered and died in some remote and mythical period of pre-history. The Christian story, on the other hand, starts off briskly in St Matthew's account with a place and a date: 'When Jesus was born in Bethlehem of Judæa in the days of Herod the King'. St Luke, still more practically and prosaically, pins the thing down by a reference to a piece of government finance. God, he says, was made man in the year when Cæsar Augustus was taking a census in connection with a scheme of taxation. Similarly, we might date an event by saying that it took place in the year that Great Britain went off the gold standard. About thirty-three years later (we are informed) God was executed, for being a political nuisance, 'under Pontius Pilate' – much as we might say, 'when Mr. Joynson-Hicks was Home Secretary'. It is as definite and concrete as all that.

Possibly we might prefer not to take this tale too seriously – there are disquieting points about it. Here we had a man of Divine character walking and talking among us – and what did we find to do with Him? The common people, indeed, 'heard Him gladly'; but our leading authorities in Church and State considered that He talked too much and uttered too many disconcerting truths. So we bribed one of His friends to hand Him over quietly to the police, and we tried Him on a rather vague charge of creating a disturbance, and had Him publicly flogged and hanged on the common gallows, 'thanking God we were rid of a knave'. All this was not very creditable to us, even if He was (as many people thought and think) only a harmless crazy preacher. But if the Church is right about Him, it was more discreditable still; for the man we hanged was God Almighty.

So that is the outline of the official story – the tale of the time when God was the under-dog and got beaten, when He submitted to the conditions He had laid down and became a man like the men He had made, and the men He had made broke Him and killed Him. This is the dogma we find so dull – this terrifying drama of which God is the victim and hero.

116

If this is dull, then what, in Heaven's name, is worthy to be called exciting? The people who hanged Christ never, to do them justice, accused Him of being a bore – on the contrary; they thought Him too dynamic to be safe. It has been left for later generations to muffle up that shattering personality and surround Him with an atmosphere of tedium. We have very efficiently pared the claws of the Lion of Judah, certified Him 'meek and mild', and recommended Him as a fitting household pet for pale curates and pious old ladies. To those who knew Him, however, He in no way suggested a milk-and-water person; *they* objected to Him as a dangerous firebrand. True, He was tender to the unfortunate, patient with honest inquirers and humble before Heaven; but He insulted respectable clergymen by calling them hypocrites; He referred to King Herod as 'that fox'; He went to parties in disreputable company and was looked upon as a 'gluttonous man and a wine-bibber, a friend of publicans and sinners'; He assaulted indignant tradesmen and threw them and their belongings out of the Temple; He drove a coach-and-horses through a number of sacrosanct and hoary regulations; He cured diseases by any means that came handy, with a shocking casualness in the matter of other people's pigs and property; He showed no proper deference for wealth or social position; when confronted with neat dialectical traps, He displayed a paradoxical humour that affronted serious-minded people, and He retorted by asking disagreeably searching questions that could not be answered by rule of thumb. He was emphatically not a dull man in His human lifetime, and if He was God, there can be nothing dull about God either. But He had 'a daily beauty in His life that made us ugly', and officialdom felt that the established order of things would be more secure without Him. So they did away with God in the name of peace and quietness.

'*And the third day He rose again*'; what are we to make of that? One thing is certain: if He was God and nothing else, His immortality means nothing to us; if He was man and no more, His death is no more important than yours or mine. But if He really was both God and man, then when the man Jesus died, God died too, and when the God Jesus rose from the dead, man rose too, because they were one and the same person. The Church binds us to no theory about the exact composition of Christ's Resurrection Body. A body of some kind there had to be, since man cannot perceive the Infinite otherwise than in terms of space and time. It may have been made from the same elements as the body that disappeared so strangely from the guarded tomb, but it was not that old, limited, mortal body, though it was recognisably like it. In any case, those who saw the risen Christ remained persuaded that life was worth living and death a triviality – an attitude curiously unlike that of the modern defeatist, who is firmly persuaded that life is a disaster and death (rather inconsistently) a major catasrophe.

Now, nobody is compelled to believe a single word of this remarkable story. God (says the Church) has created us perfectly free to disbelieve in Him as much as we choose. If we do disbelieve, then He and we must take the consequences in a world ruled by cause and effect. The Church says further, that man did, in fact, disbelieve, and that God did, in fact, take the consequences. All the same, if we are going to disbelieve a thing, it seems on the whole to be desirable that we should first find out what, exactly, we are disbelieving. Very well, then: 'The right Faith is, that we believe that Jesus Christ is God *and* Man. Perfect God and perfect Man, of a reasonable soul and human flesh subsisting. Who although He be God and Man, yet is He not two, but one Christ.' There is the essential doctrine, of which the whole elaborate structure of Christian faith and morals is only the logical consequence.

Now, we may call that doctrine exhilarating or we may call it devastating; we may call it revelation or we may call it rubbish; but if we call it dull, then words have no meaning at all. That God should play the tyrant over man is a dismal story of unrelieved oppression; that man should play the tyrant over man is the usual dreary record of human futility; but that man should play the tyrant over God and find Him a better man than himself is an astonishing drama indeed. Any journalist, hearing of it for the first time, would recognise it as News; those who did hear it for the first time actually called it News, and good news at that; though we are apt to forget that the word Gospel ever meant anything so sensational.

Perhaps the drama is played out now, and Jesus is safely dead and buried. Perhaps. It is ironical and entertaining to consider that once at least in the world's history those words might have been spoken with complete conviction, and that was upon the eve of the Resurrection.

'The Greatest Drama Ever Staged', CC pp. 1–6

The Triumph of Easter

All of us, perhaps, are too ready, when our behaviour turns out to have appalling consequences, to rush out and hang ourselves. Sometimes we do worse, and show an inclination to go and hang other people. Judas, at least, seems to have blamed nobody but himself, and St Peter, who had a minor betrayal of his own to weep for, made his act of contrition and waited to see what came next. What came next for St Peter and the other disciples was the sudden assurance of what God was, and with it the answer to all the riddles.

If Christ could take evil and suffering and do that sort of thing with them, then of course it was all worth while, and the triumph of Easter linked up with that strange, triumphant prayer in the Upper Room, which the events of Good Friday had seemed to make so puzzling. As for their own parts in the drama, nothing could now alter the fact that they had been stupid, cowardly, faithless, and in many ways singularly unhelpful; but they did not allow any morbid and egotistical remorse to inhibit their joyful activities in the future.

Now, indeed, they could go out and 'do something' about the problem of sin and suffering. They had seen the strong hands of God twist the crown of thorns into a crown of glory, and in hands as strong as that they knew themselves safe. They had misunderstood practically everything Christ had ever said to them, but no matter: the thing made sense at last, and the meaning was far beyond anything they had dreamed. They had expected a walk-over, and they beheld a victory; they had expected an earthly Messiah, and they beheld the Soul of Eternity.

It had been said to them of old time, 'No man shall look upon My face and live'; but for them a means had been found. They had seen the face of the living God turned upon them; and it was the face of a suffering and rejoicing Man.

'The Triumph of Easter', CC pp. 12–13

7

LONDON CALLING

=

This poem, on rediscovered values, comes from the heart of the war-time world and Dorothy Sayers' hope for the future, and was published in 1942 just a year before her discovery of Dante.

'Lord, I Thank Thee ——'

If it were not for the war,
This war
Would suit me down to the ground.
There are things about it which pander to my worst
    instincts,
Flatter my weak points,
And make me a prig and a Pharisee.

I have always detested travelling,
And now there is no travelling to do.
I need not feel that I ought to be improving my mind
By a visit to Rome, the Pyramids, the Pyrenees,
New York or New Guinea,
Or even Moscow;
I have never really panted to contemplate Fuji-Yama,
And now I need not bother about it;
I need not feel abashed by people who take their
    holidays on the Matterhorn
Or navigating the Fiords;

I can sit quietly in Essex and feel superior
When my friends complain
That they cannot get on without a sea-voyage, or
    sea-bathing,
(I abominate cold water),
That they feel stifled
Without a breath of mountain air.

I was born in a hollow
At a confluence of rivers,
I was brought up in a swamp
Carved, caged, counter-checked like a chessboard
By dyke and drain,
Running from the Great Ouse to the Wash,
Where the wind never stops blowing;
I know all about the smell that comes off the drowned
    land
When the waters turn home in the spring
(A peculiar smell – and I have encountered something
    like it
In Venice,
In the *piccoli canali* in the moonlight,
Where it is considered highly romantic);
I can say to the gadabouts:
'If you must have dank smells, you can get them in
    the Fens of East Anglia;
If you must break your necks on a precipice
You can do it with perfect discomfort
In Cumberland;
And there are apple-blossoms in Kent,
Blue seas on the Cornish coast,
Conifers in Scotland;
But I shall stay at home,
Indulging my natural laziness,
And save petrol and coal for my country;
And if anybody requests me
To deliver unnecessary speeches in remote parts of
    the country,
I can plead the difficulties of war-time travel,
And suffer no pangs of conscience.

I detest bananas,
A smug fruit, designed to be eaten in railway carriages
On Bank Holidays,
With a complexion like yellow wax
And a texture like new putty
Flavoured with nail-polish.
Yes, we have no bananas,
Glory be!
And the hygienic people
Who eat prunes and grape-fruit for breakfast
Are cast into outer darkness
Gnashing their dentures.
Why should anybody eat breakfast
For its edifying qualities,
Or its slimming properties;
Or its improving influence
Upon the skin and bowels?
Behold, the mortal has put on immortality,
And the last shall be first
In the economy of managed consumption.
I do not take sugar
In tea or coffee (even black coffee);
I can give it away to my neighbours,
Purchasing their grateful affection
At no cost to myself –
If everybody was made like me
The Ministry of Food would rejoice.

I need not buy new clothes,
Or change for dinner,
Or bother to make up my face –
It is virtuous to refrain from these things.
I need not shiver in silk stockings; –
I had a hunch about wool before it was rationed;
Now I have knitted myself woollen stockings
That come a long way up.
They are warm and admirable,
They do not ladder or go into holes suddenly.
I can boast quietly about them
And smirk while others admire my industry;

As it happens, I like knitting
And nothing gratifies one more
Than to be admired for doing what one likes.
In London there are still shops
With silk stockings in the windows
('Positively the last release');
I see the women and the girls
Check in their stride, stop, gaze in hungrily,
Fumbling with handbags, calculating coupons,
Yielding to temptation.
Poor souls!
They will never be able to walk through the rose-garden
Or play with the kitten
But anxiety will gnaw at their hearts like a demon rat;
The crack of a snapping stitch
Will sound in their ears like the crack of doom.
But I shall walk cheerfully in woollen
This winter, and the next, and the next,
Hand-knitted without coupons;
And the old lisle stockings will do for the summer –
If there is any summer.

It is jolly to take up a newspaper
And find it so thin!
The ruthless restriction of twaddle
Is a rare, refreshing fruit
Better than many bananas.
The Woman's Page,
The Sports Page,
The Feature Page,
The Page of Bathing Beauties,
Are clipped as close as Samson's skull,
Together with the Comic Strip
And the God-wottery Corner for Garden-lovers.
The blare of the advertisements,
Imploring, cajoling, stimulating, menacing, terrifying
An apathetic public
Into buying what it neither needs nor desires,
Has dwindled into an apologetic murmur,
Regretting the shortage of supplies,

Whispering pathetically, 'Forget-me-not,
Forget me not when good times come again!'
We are not electrified every other day
By the bursting into the world,
With accompaniments suitable to the advent of a long-
    promised Messiah,
Of a new soap.
Soap is rationed.
(I always thought we washed far too much anyhow –
Animals do not wear out their skins
And destroy their natural oils
With perpetual washing;
Even the cat despises soap,
And who ever heard of a cow washing behind the ears?)
There is very little room these days
For the misreporting of my public utterances;
Soon they will not be reported at all,
Thank goodness!
And, curiously enough, books and plays seem to do better
When nobody reviews them.
Also, owing to the lack of paper
The demand for books exceeds the supply –
A thing that has not been known
Since they started all this popular education and cheap
    printing.
Nobody ever wants a thing
Until it is taken away –
We used to have far too much of everything.

I can now enjoy a more glorious victory,
More exaltation of spirit,
By capturing a twopenny tin of mustard
Or a packet of hairpins
And bearing it home in triumph
Than I could have achieved before the war
By securing a First Folio of Shakespeare
At vast trouble and expense
In the sale-room.
The local chimney-sweep
Keeps hens.

He takes the scraps from my table, the kitchen scraps,
And the hens return them to me,
By a beautiful economy of nature,
In the likeness of eggs.
A new-laid egg
Will bind a friendship
Faster than it binds a cake;
A string of onions
Is a gift more gracious
Than a necklace of pearls;
I am better off with vegetables
At the bottom of my garden
Than with all the fairies of the *Midsummer Night's Dream.*

If it were not for the war,
This war
Would suit me down to the ground.

LC pp. 293–8

In an essay on 'The Other Six Deadly Sins' Dorothy Sayers was acute in identifying some questions to be asked about the post-war world. She enquired what would happen to us when the war machine ceased to consume our surplus products for us. She wondered whether we would hold fast our rediscovered sense of real values and our adventurous attitude to life, or whether we would again 'allow our Gluttony to become the instrument of an economic system which thrives upon waste and rubbish heaps'.

. . . At present the waste (that is, sheer gluttonous consumption) is being done for us in the field of war. In peace, if we do not revise our ideas, we shall ourselves become its instruments. The rubbish-heap will again be piled on our own doorsteps, on our own backs, in our own bellies. Instead of the wasteful consumption of trucks and tanks, metal and explosives, we shall have back the wasteful consumption of wireless sets and silk stockings, drugs and paper, cheap pottery and cosmetics – all the slop and swill that pour down the sewers over which the palace of Gluttony is built.

Gluttony is warm-hearted. It is the excess and perversion of that free, careless, and generous mood which desires to enjoy life and to see others enjoy it. But, like Lust and Wrath, it is a headless, heedless sin, that puts the good-natured person at the mercy of the cold head and the cold heart; and these exploit it and bring it to judgment, so that at length it issues in its own opposite – in that very 'dearth in the midst of plenty' at which we stand horrified to-day.

In especial, it is at the mercy of the sin called *Avaritia* or *Covetousness*. At one time this sin was content to call itself 'Honest Thrift', and under that name was, as they might say in Aberdeen, 'varra weel respectit'. The cold-hearted sins recommend themselves to Church and State by the restraints they lay upon the vulgar and disreputable warm-hearted sins. The thrifty poor do not swill beer in pubs, or indulge in noisy quarrels in the streets to the annoyance of decent people – moreover, they are less likely to become a burden on the rates. The thrifty well-to-do do not abash their pious neighbours by lavish indulgence in Gula or Luxuria – which are both very expensive sins. Nevertheless, there used always to be certain reservations about the respect accorded to Covetousness. It was an unromantic, unspectacular sin. Unkind people sometimes called it by rude names, such as Parsimony and Niggardliness. It was a narrow, creeping, pinched kind of sin; and it was not a good mixer. It was more popular with Caesar than with Caesar's subjects; it had no glamour about it.

It was left for the present age to endow Covetousness with glamour on a big scale, and to give it a title which it could carry like a flag. It occurred to somebody to call it Enterprise. From the moment of that happy inspiration, Covetousness has gone forward and never looked back. It has become a swaggering, swashbuckling, piratical sin, going about with its hat cocked over its eye, and with pistols tucked into the tops of its jack-boots. Its war-cries are 'Business Efficiency!' 'Free Competition!' 'Get Out or Get Under!' and 'There's Always Room at the Top!' It no longer screws and saves – it launches out into new enterprises; it gambles and speculates; it thinks in a big way; it takes risks. It can no longer be troubled to deal in real wealth, and so remain attached to Work and the Soil. It has set money free from all such hampering ties; it has interests in every continent; it is impossible to pin it down to any one place or any concrete commodity – it is an adventurer, a roving, rollicking free-lance. It looks so jolly and jovial, and has such a twinkle in its cunning eye, that nobody can believe that its heart is as cold and calculating as ever. Besides, where is its heart? Covetousness is not incarnated in individual people, but in business corporations, joint-stock companies, amalgamations, trusts, which have neither bodies to be kicked, nor souls to be damned – nor hearts to be appealed to, either. It is very difficult to fasten on anybody the responsibility for the things that are done with money. Of course, if Covetousness miscalculates and some big financier comes crashing down, bringing all the small speculators down with him, we wag self-righteous heads, and feel that we see clearly where the fault lies. But we do not punish the fraudulent business-man for his frauds, but for his failure.

The Church says Covetousness is a deadly sin – but does she really think so? Is she ready to found Welfare Societies to deal with financial immorality as she does with sexual immorality? Do the officials stationed at church doors in Italy to exclude women with bare arms turn anybody away on the grounds that they are too well-dressed to be honest? Do the vigilance committees who complain of 'suggestive' books and plays make any attempt to suppress the literature which 'suggests' that getting on in the world is the chief object in life? Is Dives, Like Magdalen, ever refused the sacraments on the grounds that he, like her, is an 'open and notorious evil-liver'? Does the Church arrange services with bright congregational singing, for Total Abstainers from Usury?

The Church's record is not, in these matters, quite as good as it might be. But is perhaps rather better than that of those who denounce her for her neglect. The Church is not the Vatican, nor the Metropolitans, nor the Bench of Bishops; it is not even the Vicar or the Curate or the Church-wardens: the Church is you and I. And are you and I in the least sincere in our pretence that we disapprove of Covetousness?

Let us ask ourselves one or two questions. Do we admire and envy rich people because they are rich, or because the work by which they made their money is good work? If we hear that Old So-and-so has pulled off a pretty smart deal with the Town Council, are we shocked by the revelation of the cunning graft involved, or do we say admiringly: 'Old So-and-so's hot stuff – you won't find many flies on him'? When we go to the cinema and see a picture about empty-headed people in luxurious surroundings, do we say: 'What drivel!' or do we sit in a misty dream, wishing we could give up our daily work and marry into surroundings like that? When we invest our money, do we ask ourselves whether the enterprise represents anything useful, or merely whether it is a safe thing that returns a good dividend? Do we regularly put money into football pools or dog-racing? When we read the newspaper, are our eyes immediately arrested by anything which says 'MILLIONS' in large capitals, preceded by the £ or $ sign? Have we ever refused money on the grounds that the work that we had to do for it was something that we could not do honestly, or do well? Do we NEVER choose our acquaintance with the idea that they are useful people to know, or keep in with people in the hope that there is something to be got out of them? And do we – this is important – when we blame the mess that the economical world has got into, do we always lay the blame on wicked financiers, wicked profiteers, wicked capitalists, wicked employers, wicked bankers – or do we sometimes ask ourselves how far *we* have contributed to make the mess?

'The Other Six Deadly Sins', CC pp. 74–7

128

The sixth Deadly Sin is named by the Church *Acedia* or *Sloth*. In the world it calls itself Tolerance; but in hell it is called Despair. It is the accomplice of the other sins and their worst punishment. It is the sin which believes in nothing, cares for nothing, seeks to know nothing, interferes with nothing, enjoys nothing, loves nothing, hates nothing, finds purpose in nothing, lives for nothing, and only remains alive because there is nothing it would die for. We have known it far too well for many years. The only thing perhaps that we have not known about it is that it is mortal sin.

The war has jerked us pretty sharply into consciousness about this slug-a-bed sin of Sloth, and perhaps we need not say too much about it. But two warnings are rather necessary.

First, it is one of the favourite tricks of this Sin to dissemble itself under cover of a whiffling activity of body. We think that if we are busily rushing about and doing things, we cannot be suffering from Sloth. And besides, violent activity seems to offer an escape from the horrors of Sloth. So the other sins hasten to provide a cloak for Sloth: Gluttony offers a whirl of dancing, dining, sports, and dashing very fast from place to place to gape at beauty spots; which when we get to them, we defile with vulgarity and waste. Covetousness rakes us out of bed at an early hour, in order that we may put pep and hustle into our business: Envy sets us to gossip and scandal, to writing cantakerous letters to the papers, and to the unearthing of secrets and the scavenging of dustbins; Wrath provides (very ingeniously) the argument that the only fitting activity in a world so full of evil-doers and evil demons is to curse loudly and incessantly: 'Whatever brute and blackguard made the world'; while Lust provides that round of dreary promiscuity that passes for bodily vigour. But these are all disguises for the empty heart and the empty brain and the empty soul of Acedia.

Let us take particular notice of the empty brain. Here Sloth is in a conspiracy with Envy to prevent people from thinking. Sloth persuades us that stupidity is not our sin, but our misfortune; while Envy at the same time persuades us that intelligence is despicable – a dusty, highbrow, and commercially useless thing.

And secondly, the War has jerked us out of Sloth; but wars, if they go on very long, induce Sloth in the shape of war-weariness and despair of any purpose. We saw its effects in the last peace, when it brought all the sins in its train. There are times when one

129

is tempted to say that the great, sprawling, lethargic sin of Sloth is the oldest and greatest of the sins and the parent of all the rest.

'The Other Six Deadly Sins', CC pp 84–5

Her own antidote to Gluttony, Covetousness and Sloth she published in an essay on 'Vocation in Work', also addressed to the post-war world of which she would be a part. And it makes some good points about 'creatively working women' too. It is printed in its entirety.

Vocation in Work

The sense of a Divine vocation must be restored to a man's daily work.

In December 1940 the leaders of the Churches in Britain put forward as one of the points necessary for the reconstruction of society: 'That the sense of Divine vocation must be restored to a man's daily work'. By thus lifting the subject of labour out of the sphere of economics, and calling for a sacramental relation between man and his work, they were courageously grappling with a problem which too many 'social planners' have scandalously neglected.

Since the break with the Catholic tradition in the fifteenth century, religious opinion in the Reformed Churches has relied for guidance chiefly upon the text of the Canonical Scriptures. Oddly enough, apart from one very noble passage in the Apocrypha, the Scriptures are not very explicit on the subject of work; and I think that our feeling about it may have been too strongly influenced by an unimaginative interpretation of the famous passage in Genesis about the curse of Adam. 'Cursed is the ground for thy sake; thorns also and thistles shall bring it forth to thee: in the sweat of thy face shalt thou eat bread.'

Work, it seemed, was a curse and a punishment; perhaps this encouraged men to feel that no blessing and no sacrament could be associated with it. Yet the whole of Christian doctrine centres round the great paradox of redemption, which asserts that the very pains and sorrows by which fallen man is encompassed can become the instruments of his salvation, if they are accepted and transmuted by love. 'O blessed sin,' says the Ambrosian liturgy boldly, 'that didst merit such and so great a Redeemer.' The first Adam was cursed with labour and suffering; the redemption of labour and suffering is the triumph of the second Adam – the Carpenter nailed to the cross.

We ought, perhaps, to look a little more closely at that profound and poetic myth of the creation and fall of man. 'God', says the writer, 'made man in his own image – in the image of God created he him; male and female created he them.' And the first thing he tells us about God, in whose image both man and woman were created, is that He was Himself a Creator. He made things. Not, presumably, because He had to, but because He wanted to. He made light and water, and earth and birds, and fish and animals, and enjoyed what He had done. And then He made man 'in his own image' – a creature in the image of a Creator. And there is indeed one thing which is quite distinctive about man: he makes things – not just one uniform set of necessary things, as a bee makes honey-comb, but an interminable variety of different and not strictly necessary things, because he wants to. Even in this fallen and unsatisfactory life, man is still so near His divine pattern that he continually makes things, as God makes things, for the fun of it. He is *homo faber* – man the craftsman – and this is the point from which I want to set out. Man is a maker, who makes things because he wants to, because he cannot fulfil his true nature if he is prevented from making things for the love of the job; he is made in the image of the Maker, and he must himself create or become something less than a man.

Can we really believe that the writer of Genesis supposed the unfallen happiness of Adam and Eve to consist in an interminable idleness? If so, a study of the tale itself will correct that idea – the poet imagined for man no such hell of unmitigated boredom. Adam was put in the garden of Eden 'to dress and till it', and for intellectual occupation he had the surely very enjoyable task of naming all the animals. What, then, in the writer's mind, was the really operative part of the curse? The work was to be more difficult, certainly – there were to be thorns and thistles – but there was to be something else as well. Work was to be conditioned by economic necessity – that was the new and ominous thing. 'In the sweat of thy face *shalt thou eat bread.*' And here we may look at what the materialist dogma of communism has said about man's nature: 'Man is first man when he produces the means of livelihood.' *The means of livelihood.* To the assertion, 'Man is only man when he produces (or makes),' the Christian may readily assent: for that is the Adam made in the image of God. But when the words 'the means of livelihood' are added, they rivet upon the essential nature of man the judgment of man's corruption: 'economic man' is Adam under the curse. The economic factor in human society is, of course, a reality, as sin and pain and sorrow and every other human evil are realities; and it is the duty of Christians to accept and redeem those real evils. But to assume, as we have increasingly allowed ourselves to assume of late years

– to assume, as so many well-intentioned architects of an improved society assume today – that economics is the sole basis of man's dealing with nature and with his fellow-men, is the very negation of all Christian principle. This assumption is rooted in a lie; it is a falsehood that runs counter to the law of human nature; and like everything that runs counter to the nature of things, it can only lead to the judgment of catastrophe. For this reason it is impossible that the economic situation should ever be rightly adjusted so long as it is looked upon as being *merely* an economic question. To get the economic situation dealt with we must lift it out of the economic sphere altogether, and consider first what is the right relation between the work itself and the worker, who is made in the image of the eternal Craftsman.

Now, this point of view, which a few centuries ago would have been a commonplace, is today almost inconceivably remote from the ideas of the ordinary man. It appears to him to be a kind of theoretical luxury, out of all relation to the facts of life. He will ask, How can we indulge in any such high-falutin romance about work until we have gained a measure of economic security? And again, How can men hope to enjoy their work creatively when most of it is so distasteful that they can only be induced to do it by the necessity for earning a livelihood? The answer to this is one which it is almost impossible to get people to understand: namely, that it is precisely the concentration upon economic security which makes both security and enjoyment in work unattainable, because it is a setting up of the means to an end as an end-in-itself, so that the true end and object of work is lost and forgotten.

Let us for a moment consider a group of workers who have never – in spite of much incidental corruption – altogether abandoned the divine conception of what work ought to be. They are people whose way of life is, in essentials, so sharply distinguished from that of the ordinary worker that the designers of economic Utopias can find no place for them, and will scarcely allow them to be workers at all. Economic society has grown so far away from them that it views them with suspicion as mysterious aliens, does its best to push them out of the control of practical affairs, and is usually contemptuous and hostile at the very sound of their name. These men and women have become, as it were, an enclosed community, cut off from the world – which is bad for the world and bad for them. It is not that the working world does not see and hear plenty of them – as indeed it sees and hears and gossips about the animals in the Zoo; but always with the iron bars of misunderstanding set up between. This odd, alien community is that of the men and women who live by and for the works of the creative imagination – the people whom we lump together under the general name of 'artists'.

The great primary contrast between the artist and the ordinary worker is this: the worker works to make money, so that he may enjoy those things in life which are not his work and which his work can purchase for him; but the artist makes money by his work in order that he may go on working. The artist does not say: 'I must work in order to live'; but 'I must contrive to make money so that I may live to work'. For the artist there is no distinction between work and living: his work *is* his life, and the whole of his life – not merely the material world about him, or the colours and sounds and events that he perceives, but also all his own personality and emotions, the *whole* of his life – is the actual material of his work.

Consider the great barrier that this forges between himself and the economic worker, in quite practical and mundane ways. For example, it would be preposterous for a genuine artist to submit himself to strict trade-union rules. How could he agitate for an eight-hour day or keep to it if he got it? There is no moment in the twenty-four hours when he can truthfully say he is not working. The emotions, the memories, the sufferings, the dreams even of the periods when he is not actually at his desk or his easel – these are his stuff and his tools; and his periods of leisure are the periods when his creative imagination may be most actively at work. He cannot say, 'Here work stops and leisure begins'; he cannot stop work unless he stops living. Or how could he, in his own financial interests or those of his fellows, adopt the policy of keeping his work, in speed or quality, down to the level of the slowest or stupidest of his colleagues? Mr. Bernard Shaw is a Socialist, but I cannot see him scaling down his standards to the level of a writer in *Peg's Paper*, even to establish the principle of the basic minimum wage for writers. Some things the artist will indeed do for the economic security of his weaker brethren – he will, for example, agree to use a certain amount of genteel blackmail upon publishers in the matter of contracts and copyright. But any limitation upon his right to work himself to death if he chooses, or to choose the kind of work he will do, that he will resist to his last breath, for to set fetters upon his work is to set fetters upon his life.

There is a price paid for the artist's freedom, as for all freedom. He, of all workers in the world, has the least economic security. The money value of his work is at the mercy of every wind of public opinion; and if he falls by the wayside he cannot claim unemployment benefit, or look to the State to pay doctor's bills, educate his children and compensate him for injuries incurred in the exercise of his profession. If he falls off a cliff while painting a picture, if he loses his wits or suffers a failure of invention, society will not hold itself responsible; nor, if his publisher suddenly decides to be rid of him, can he sue the man for wrongful dismissal. Moreover, he is taxed with a singular injustice; while the world pays tribute to his unworldliness by expecting him to place a great deal of his time, energy and stock-in-trade at the disposal of the community without payment. The artist puts up with these disabilities because his way of life is not primarily rooted in economics. True, he often demands high prices for his work – but he wants the money not in order that he may stop working and go away and do something different, but in order that he may indulge in the luxury of doing some part of his work for nothing. 'Thank heaven,' the artist will say, 'I've made enough with that book, or play, or picture of mine, to take a couple of years off *to do my own work*' – by which he probably means some book or play or picture which will cost him an immense amount of labour and pains and which he has very little chance of selling. In fact, when the artist rejoices because he has been relieved from the pressure of economic necessity he means that he has been relieved – not from the work, but from the money.

Now, this is not merely because the artist is his own master, working for himself and not for an employer. The same thing holds good of the actor, for example, who is quite literally an employed person – who can actually draw unemployment benefit. The actor, like other artists, passionately enjoys doing work for nothing or next to nothing, if only he can afford to do it. And he never talks of himself as 'employed'; if he is employed, he tells you that he is 'working'.

I think we can measure the distance we have fallen from the idea that work is a vocation to which we are called, by the extent to

135

which we have come to substitute the word 'employment' for 'work'. We say we must solve the 'problem of unemployment' – we reckon up how many 'hands' are 'employed'; our social statistics are seldom based upon the work itself – whether the right people are doing it, or whether the work is worth doing. We have come to set a strange value on leisure for its own sake – not the leisure which enables a man to get on properly with his job, but the leisure which is a polite word for idleness. The commodities which it is easiest to advertise and sell are those which purport to 'take the work out' of everything – the tinned foods that need no cooking – the clothes that wash themselves – the switches and gadgets that save time and make leisure. Which would be grand if we eagerly needed that extra time and leisure in order to make and do things. Alas! the commodities easiest to sell after the labour-saving gadgets are the inventions for saving us from the intolerable leisure we have produced, and for painlessly killing the time we have saved. The entertainment to which we can passively listen, the game we can watch without taking part in it, the occupation, however meaningless, which can relieve us from the trouble of thinking. As a result, far too many people in this country seem to go about only half alive. All their existence is an effort to escape from what they are doing. And the inevitable result of this is a boredom, a lack of purpose, a passivity which eats life away at the heart, and a disillusionment which prompts men to ask what life is all about, and complain with only too much truth, that they can 'make nothing of it'.

Now that the Churches are setting themselves to tackle this dislocation that has weakened our grip upon work I think they will find in it the root cause of a great many other evils – evils that they have failed to cure directly because they were treating the symptoms rather than the disease. It is, for instance, passivity, lack of purpose, and a failure to discharge pent-up creative energy into daily work that drives a civilisation into that bored and promiscuous sexuality which derives not from excess of vitality, but from lack of something better to do, and which is always the mark of a civilisation which has lost sight of true purpose in its work.

Or again: the appearance of a parasitic and exploiting class is closely connected with a way of life deficient in opportunities for creative activity. In this connection, both Churches and secular 'planners' should give some attention to what is known as the 'woman's question' – an important subject usually ignored in the schemes for a 'new order'.

In this war, as in the last, the women are being called upon to come out of their homes and do, as we say, 'the men's work'. They come, and they do it, and everybody says how splendid they are. But the offers of work to them are usually accompanied with the warning that after the war the men will have to come back to their jobs – and, indeed, I notice a very strong tendency, both on the Left and on the Right, to suggest that when the crisis is past the women are to be pushed out of the trades and professions and restored as far as possible, to their homes, in the interests of 'employment'.

I see the men's point of view about this. I understand the resentment against the women who 'take the men's jobs'. But it should be realised that, under modern conditions, the opportunities for intelligent *work* afforded by the home are very greatly restricted, compared with what they were, and that many of the women's traditional jobs have, since the age of mechanical industry began, been filched from them by the men. The baking industry, the whole of the nation's spinning, weaving and dyeing, the breweries, the distilleries, the confectionery, the preserving curing and pickling of food, the perfumery, the lace-making, the dairying, the cheese-making, have been transferred from the home to the factory, and the control and management – the intelligent part of them – handed over to men. It was the commercial age that presented us with a class of really leisured women – pampered and exploiting women, with no creative job to which they might set hand and brain. It was then that the possession of an idle woman became the hallmark of a man's success; and it is dangerous when – through a vast reserve either of slave-labour as in ancient Rome or of machine-labour as in modern Europe – idleness becomes an ideal attainable by a vast mass of citizens. Because an idle and a bored class is bound to be a parasitic and exploiting class. Men cannot live for their work if they are harassed by an army of empty-minded women demanding that they should work in order to get money to support a decorative idleness. We cannot now, of course, restore to the home everything that machines and commerce have taken from it. But I ask the Churches, and I ask all social reformers, to take seriously this warning that they cannot

137

have a society of creatively-working and unexploited men unless they can also arrange for a society of creatively working women without the temptation to become exploiters of men's labour.

At this point, of course, we come up against a really fundamental difficulty. It is all very well for the artist to talk like this, but *his* work is of a really creative and satisfying kind. That is why he doesn't want to get away from it. But how about the factory-hand whose work consists of endlessly and monotonously pushing a pin into a slot? How can he be expected to live for the sake of the work? Isn't he right to want to make money so as to get away from it as quickly as possible? Can you blame him for looking on work as 'employment' – as something to be done grudgingly, with as little exertion as possible? Doesn't it correspond to the artist's necessary 'pot-boiler', which has to be ground out in order that he may get away to 'his own work'? It is useless and silly to say that machines and industry ought to be abolished. We can't turn time backwards. We have to cope with things as they are and make the best of them. This is what the worker will always retort when you talk to him about the sense of vocation in work. Well, that is so; and unless and until we can achieve a radical change in our whole attitude to work and money, we shall have to allow that a great deal of necessary work *is* in the nature of a pot-boiler, and that it ought to be arranged so as to boil the pot as quickly as possible and in such a way that nobody's pot remains without a fire to boil it. This is the task on which those reformers are engaged who try to deal with the question in purely economic terms. And while we have to deal with it along those lines, we may take the opportunity of trying to establish two things: First that even work done for pot-boiling should be done as well and as conscientiously as possible. Secondly, that when the pot-boiling is done the worker should be taught and encouraged to turn to 'his own work' – to some creative and satisfying hobby at least; and not merely to an idle and soul-deadening killing of time. But these things are at best palliatives. They do not get to the root of the matter, which is the nation-wide and world-wide acceptance of a false scale of values about work, money, and leisure.

First of all, is there anything whatever that will not only reconcile the worker to even the most monotonous and soul-killing kind of toil, but also make him ready to undertake it with eagerness and a kind of passionate satisfaction?

138

The enthusiasm with which labour went to work after the Dunkirk disaster and during the 'Tanks-for-Russia' week suggests that the power that enables men to work with enthusiasm is a real conviction of the worth of their work. They will endure much if, like the artist, they passionately desire to see the job completed and to know that it is very good. But what are we to say about a civilisation which employs so many of its workers in doing work which has no worth at all, work which no living man with a soul in him could desire to see, work which has nothing whatever to justify it, *except* the manufacture of employment and the creation of profits? *That* is the real vicious circle in which we are all enclosed. *That* is the real indictment we have to bring against a commercial age. And it is one which we cannot meet by the adjustment of wages, or by the restriction of private enterprise, or by the transference of capital from the individual to the State.

It is not within my knowledge or capacity to deal with the machinery of economic adjustments. I have not the special knowledge that would enable me to make suggestions about world-matters or the movements of money upon the exchanges. And in any case, I am convinced that *no* satisfactory adjustment of these things can ever be made without a radical alteration in the attitude of everybody – not merely 'the worker', but *everybody* – to this matter of the worth of the work. Unless we are regenerate and born again, we cannot enter into the kingdom of a divine understanding of work. It is not enough to repeat 'from each according to his ability and to each according to his need'. That leaves out the very centre of the question. *What* is each man to provide? *What* does each man need? You must decide that before you can decide how to requisition and distribute it. There should be work for all – certainly. But what kind of work is it to be? That is the kind of question which appears only too seldom on the programmes for the 'reorientation of society'.

If, keeping this question in our minds as we go about, we look at some of the commodities our civilisation has produced, we may easily begin to wonder how on earth we can possibly expect the makers of them to feel any satisfaction in their work. It is no wonder if, in making them, they think only of the money they represent in wages and profits. There are two things we may mean when we say, 'this thing is mine' – that we own it (as when we say, 'my car', 'my boots', 'my vacuum cleaner') or that we made

139

it, as when the painter says, 'that is my picture' – even though it may have passed into the ownership of the man who bought it. So the man who has laid the bricks of a beautiful house might be proud to say, 'that house is mine, for I made it,' even though he can never hope to own such a house himself. But there are other houses in making which no one could feel any pride or satisfaction – houses not only ugly but shoddy, not even well-designed for the most utilitarian purpose which a house can serve. They are the houses whose value is only reckoned in money; wage-and-profit houses, in which neither landlord, nor architect, nor builder, nor labourer can feel any human pride and satisfaction or the owners any human affection – how could any bricklayer be blamed for laying his bricks as slowly as possible if *that* is all this his work is to produce in the end? Or consider the mountains of tasteless and useless clutter which which we surround ourselves – the encumbrances which nobody really wants, which people have to be bullied and nagged and seduced into thinking they want by an incessant clamour of advertising propaganda; things which exist only to use up the waste products of commerce and manufacture work and wages to keep the machines running – consider them, and ask whether men made in the image of God can or should be required to dedicate their lives to the production of all this junk of china dogs, patent medicines, telephone-dolls, nail-varnishes, crooner-music, trash novels, and general rubbish and nonsense with which commerce has cluttered the world.

There is worse than this: there is the work which is forced to be bad work ill done, because to do it well would bring down profits and spoil the market. The worker may not make that good gramophone, that well-constructed chair, that perfectly engineered machine that would give him satisfaction in the making. He must make something guaranteed to get out of order quickly, so that it may be superseded by something else. He must not work for the worth of the work itself, but only to keep the machines running and to make new opportunities for profit and employment. And before we blame either employer or worker for this state of things, let us ask ourselves whether we do not all contribute to it by always demanding the newest thing, by our snobbery of the modern and the up-to-date, by our ignorance and carelessness about how things work, and our inability to distinguish good craftsmanship from bad. Let us remember also that again and

140

again the really useful and really good invention is thought out and patented only to be bought up by a manufacturer and suppressed because it is too good – it would throw all his other manufactures off the market. The consumer does not realise how the economic society in which he acquiesces actually forbids him to use and enjoy the things which the creative mind invents for his delight and convenience. He is not allowed to have these things – they would interfere with the scramble for profits and wages. As for the inventor, the work of his creative mind is simply taken away from him and killed dead. If he is lucky, he has been given a sum of money to compensate him. By a cynical fiction he is supposed to be satisfied, because he has been paid – as one is paid and compensated for the loss of one's limbs or one's children in a road accident. Whether or not it creates profit for the employer, and whether or not it creates employment for the worker, such a way of dealing with the work itself is vile and evil; the salvation of society cannot lie that way.

Whenever economics is put first, the worth of the work suffers, and man's creative delight in his work is destroyed and his sense of vocation lost. Restriction of production by the employer is balanced by ca'canny among the trade unions; whoever is bene-fited, it is always the work that suffers, and when the work is degraded the heart is taken out of the worker.

What we have to beware of here is the corruption that lies hidden in the best of human good. It seems reasonable and just to say that rights of humanity should be considered before the right of the *thing* – the right of the work itself. A man has a right to subsistence – *therefore* he should be employed on something, even if it is only on nonsense, *therefore* he should be paid according to the needs of his family, whether his work is well done or not. But if, as I maintain, the opportunity to work well and rejoice in his work turns out to be a primary human need, what then? Any satisfaction that the worker gains is founded in frustration.

After the last war we gave men money to stand idle. What was the objection to making them build houses, roads, bridges, till the land, undertake works of public utility for the money we paid them? Well, we were told that to do this would upset the whole machinery of commercialism, that the state building and engineer-ing would conflict with the vested interests, with the labour market, with trade union regulations – that to make men work

141

for the 'dole' – a hateful word for a hateful thing – would be an infringement of their liberty. At first the men cried out in protest: they wanted to work. In the name of economic orthodoxy and the rights of economic man we killed their hope and desire to work, and gave them money instead. The next generation cried less loudly for work – it learned to refuse work, lest work should pay them less than 'the dole'. Still in the name of economic orthodoxy and the rights of economic man we penalised them for working – till in the end we almost succeeded in producing a race of men to whom work and the satisfaction of work had become impossible. Now, when such a condition is reached in any country there arises an intolerable situation, the only possible outcome of which is the judgment of war, that flings men violently back into employment and brutally cuts the Gordian knot of 'production for profit' by destroying the product and making all work unprofitable. The surplus that we refuse to give away we are forced to blow away in an orgy of sheer destruction.

We are horrified by the waste of war. Curiously enough, we are not nearly so much horrified by the waste of peace and prosperity. We are only just learning to see the wickedness of employing men to grow rubber and coffee and then destroying the crops to keep up prices; of burning tobacco that has not paid duty in 'the King's pipe' because it would be commercially unsound to find a use for it; of discouraging men from growing and making things for themselves, lest they should interfere with the tradesman's profits. A right kind of work must be related, not only to a right understanding of the needs of man, but also to a willingness to serve and love the material body of God's universe. We are fond of priding ourselves on our conquest of Nature – but we ought not to treat Nature as the Germans treat a conquered province, by spoiling, ravaging and destroying for our own greed. A truly creative society knows two kinds of value, and two only: the produce of the earth and the labour of man; all money that does not represent one of those two values is false money, whose issue will in time render society bankrupt.

It is strange that whereas this age is beginning to look like the age in which the working class will become the ruling class there was never perhaps an age in which work was less loved or less reverenced for its own sake. The worker's claim to rule is apt to be based like other claims to rule, upon the possession of force and power. To say that work is at once the most hateful and the most powerful thing in the world is a very desperate assertion. If work is to rule, then we ought to see to it that its rule is not rooted in hate and upheld by resentment. For, if it is, it will not be the rule of work – it will still be the rule of economics policed by force. If work is really to *be* work – the creative activity that can redeem the world – it must be both reverenced and rededicated.

I do not think that when this war ends we shall enter upon a period of security and stability and prosperity. I do not see how we could – and I do not think it really desirable that we should. But I do think it essential that we should somehow contrive to enter upon a period of eager, and honest, and dedicated work. A period when we shall be prepared to live hard and rough so long as the work is done; when we shall forget to think about money and think first and foremost about the true needs of man and the right handling of material things. If, when the strains and stresses of war are over, we try to let up and sink back and rest, we shall destroy ourselves. In war, work has found its soul – this time, we *must not* lose it again in peace. Instead of crying out for an 'enduring peace' we might do well to hope, not exactly for an enduring war, but for the carrying over into the strenuous times that lie ahead of that meaning which war has taught us to give to work.

I will not, as some of our prophets do, offer the slightest hope of a secure and easy time 'after the war'. I think it will be a time when we must continue to adventure forth, 'a fire on the one hand and a deep water on the other', working as we have never worked in our lives and looking to the end of the work.

'Vocation in Work', in *A Christian Basis for the Post War World* pp. 88–103

8

THE PASSIONATE
INTELLECT

=

In Dante's *Divine Comedy* Dorothy Sayers found unexpected refreshment and renewed trust in the resources of the western Latin tradition of theology as she had appropriated it. She had dipped into the reading of the *Comedy* as any of us might, but in her fifties she plunged into a reading of the whole text, as a direct result of being inspired by the work of another fine non-clerical theologian, Charles Williams, whose book on *The Figure of Beatrice* was published in 1943. As it happened, E. V. Rieu's Penguin Classics series was to begin with his own translation of Homer's *Odyssey* in 1944, so it was her great good fortune to be able to contribute to the beginnings of a remarkable publishing venture. Her translation of Dante's work appeared in three stages. The publication of *Hell* in 1949 prompted the only academic honour she received after her first degrees, a Durham D.Litt. in 1950. Some of the success of her translation is due to its appearance so soon after the appalling idiocies of a world war and to her ability in her introduction and notes to relate Dante's world to our own. Readers would take the point of saying of someone, 'If his deeds do not belie him, then in that man we behold something that is an embodied damnation':

> Literally, we may or may not believe that such a man has cut himself off from redemption; but in any case, we can scarcely be mistaken in saying: 'That man presents the image of something in civilization which will corrupt and ruin civilization; of something in myself

which (if I do not recognize and repent it) will assuredly corrupt and ruin me.'

H Introduction, pp. 15–16

And we might well be horrified by what Dante could have made of the contrast between the Lady with the Lamp and the Lady with the Lampshade-made-of-Human-Skin (H Introduction, p. 18). The publication of *Purgatory* followed in 1955, but before completing *Paradise* she turned to *The Song of Roland*, published in the year of her death, as I have already mentioned. Apart from her long-standing fascination with medieval literature and religion and what the medieval tradition had to offer to the twentieth century, it may also be that she (as it were) drew breath before tackling the last thirteen Cantos of *Paradise*, which quite apart from their subject matter (the vision of God) are themselves associated with such a profoundly moving story about their discovery by Dante's sons after his death (H Introduction, pp. 52–4).

Not only the translation of *Paradise*, but also her own introduction, commentaries and notes to the whole were unfinished. The work was brilliantly completed by Barbara Reynolds (and published in 1962), but without Dorothy Sayers' distinctive theological interpretation of the text, which had marked the first two volumes of her work on the *Comedy*. In particular, we cannot know what would have been her final view of Canto 26, in which St John questions Dante about love. Barbara Reynolds' invaluable book, *The Passionate Intellect: Dorothy L. Sayers' Encounter with Dante*, is in part an entirely justifiable plea for the republication of Dorothy Sayers' lectures on the whole process of coming to terms with Dante, addressed to both specialist and non-specialist audiences, and published in *Papers on Dante* and *Further Papers on Dante*. Barbara Reynolds' own struggles with the translation of Dante give her acute insight into Dorothy Sayers', as well as constituting evidence of a close friendship, for by 1957 the two had known one another for eleven years, and Dr Reynolds had arranged many of the Dante lectures. *The Passionate Intellect* examines the remarkable nine-month exchange of letters with Charles Williams, a correspondence that ended only with Williams' death in

1945. Dorothy Sayers' delight in her reading is revealed in these letters more than anywhere else – not surprisingly as she was writing to a trusted friend whose opinions she particularly valued. To take an example, from Canto 30 of *Paradise*:

> Pure intellectual light, fulfilled with love,
> > Love of the true Good, filled with all delight,
> > Transcending sweet delight, all sweets above.

P 30. 40–2

She asked:

> Was there ever a heaven so full of nods and becks and wreathèd smiles, so gay and dancing? or where the most abstract and intellectual kind of beatitude was so merrily expressed? Surely nobody ever so passionately *wanted* a place where everybody was kind, and courteous, or carried happiness so lightly . . . .

Reynolds p. 26

And above all, 'What a writer! God's body and bones, what a writer!' (Brabazon p. 229).

For our purposes, Barbara Reynolds' book illuminates the way in which Dorothy Sayers' reading of Dante inspired anoher Cathedral play, and one which she deemed to be the best she had written. *The Just Vengeance* was written for Lichfield Cathedral's seven hundred and fiftieth anniversary in 1946. the play is about 'coinherence' as in the saying 'Whoso will carry the Cross, the Cross shall carry him' (taken with Romans 8:22 and Colossians 1:24). The title is a phrase found first in Canto 21 of *Purgatory* and explored in *Paradise* 6:

> Herein the Living Justice maketh sweet
> > All our affections, which can never be
> > Perverted now to vice or lusts unmeet.

P 6. 121–3

More thoroughly, God's just vengeance is expounded by Beatrice to Dante in *Paradise* 7, 'With such a smile as would bring happiness/To one laid on the martyr's burning bed' (P 7. 17–18). Beatrice is expounding the argument of Anselm's

Cur Deus Homo? ('Why did God become man?'), and we must return to Dante's love for Beatrice later on. Of *The Just Vengeance*, here are Dorothy Sayers' own words:

> In form, the drama is a miracle play of Man's insufficiency and God's redemptive act, set against a background of contemporary crisis. The whole action takes place in the moment of the death of an Airman shot down during the late war. In that moment, his spirit finds itself drawn into the fellowship of his native city of Lichfield; there, being shown in an image the meaning of the Atonement, he accepts the Cross, and passes, in that act of choice, from the image to the reality.
>
> JV Introduction, p. 280

What is man?

Celebrate man, exalted in the image of man,
Strongest and weakest of things! His life is a span,
A breath – death
Creeps to him through a filter. He measures the stars,
He takes the lion, humbles the unicorn, yokes
The lightning; earth shakes with his strokes.
He makes and mars; plenty is his postillion
And famine fawns at his heels; his wheels
Extend dominion; fear is his running footman.
His sculptured monuments outlast the bones
That built them and his songs outlast their stones;
He heals what first he wounded; he wounds what he heals.
Call upon man in the time of trouble – man
Shall hear. Cry in his ear for fear.
'Save, Lord, we perish!' Cry through the hurricane,
And you shall see and hear
What help there is in the might and the image of man.

JV p. 300

The Persona Dei:
the image of truth

I the image of the Unimaginable
In the place where the Image and the Unimaged are one,
The Act of the Will, the Word of the Thought, the Son
In whom the Father's selfhood is known to Himself,
I being God and with God from the beginning
Speak to Man in the place of the Images.
You that We made for Ourself in Our own image,
Free like Us to experience good by choice,
Not of necessity, laying your will in Ours
For love's sake creaturely, to enjoy your peace,
What did you do? What did you do for Us
By what you did for yourselves in the moment of choice?
O Eve My daughter, and O My dear son Adam,
Try to understand that when you chose your will
Rather than Mine, and when you chose to know evil
In your way and not in Mine, you chose for Me.
It is My will you should know Me as I am –
But how? for you chose to know your good as evil,
Therefore the face of God is evil to you,
And you know My love as terror, My mercy as judgment,
My innocence as a sword; My naked life
Would slay you. How can you ever know Me then?
Yet know you must, since you were made for that;
Thus either way you perish. Nay, but the hands
That made you, hold you still; and since you would not
Submit to God, God shall submit to you,
Not of necessity, but free to choose
For your love's sake what you refused to Mine.
God shall be man; that which man chose for man
God shall endure, and what man chose to know
God shall know too – the experience of evil
In the flesh of man; and certainly He shall feel
Terror and judgment and the point of the sword;
And God shall see God's face set like a flint
Against Him; and man shall see the Image of God
In the image of man; and man shall show no mercy.
Truly I will bear your sin and carry your sorrow,

149

And, if you will, bring you to the tree of life,
Where you may eat, and know your evil as good,
Redeeming that first knowledge. But all this
Still at your choice, and only as you choose,
Save as you choose to let Me choose in you.

Who then will choose to be the chosen of God,
And will to bear Me that I may bear you?

JV pp. 318–9

150

The plea of the Chorus

O Mary maiden! Mary of pity!
Speak for us, Mary! Speak for a world in fear!
Mary, mother and maid, send help to the city!
Speak for us, choose for us, Mary!
. . .
All that is true in us, all we were meant to be,
The lost opportunity and the broken unity,
The dead innocence, the rejected obedience,
The forfeited chastity and the frozen charity,
The caged generosity, and the forbidden pity,
Speak in the mouth of Mary, in the name of the city!
. . .
Alpha and Omega, beginning and end,
Laid on a single head in the moment of choice!
Pray God now, pray that a woman lend
Her ear to God's, as once to the serpent's voice.

Paradise all to gain and all to lose
In the second race re-run from the old start;
What will the city do now, if a girl refuse
The weight of the glory, the seven swords in the heart?

JV pp. 319–20

The Choir sings

O Virgin Mother, daughter of thy Son,
Lowliest and loftiest of created stature,
Fixed goal to which the eternal counsels run;
Thou art that she by whom our human nature
Was so ennobled that it might become
The Creator to create Himself His creature.

JV p. 322

MARY

Good Christian people, you see, this is my Son;
Be tender to Him. It was a very long journey;
The ass was footsore before we came to Bethlehem,
And there was no room in the inn. He was born in a stable,
And I wrapped Him in linen and laid Him in the manger
Between the ox and the ass. The angels sang
And the simple shepherds worshipped; the wise kings
Brought incense and myrrh and gold. Then Herod was angry,
And sent his soldiers to kill the little children –
They died because Herod was afraid of a little child –
But we took the ass and fled away into Egypt,
And presently, when things seemed a little more safe,
Came home to the carpenter's shop at Nazareth,
Where He lived thirty years in silence and obedience.
Consider now the work and word of the Son
Before the ass carries Him up to Jerusalem.

JV p. 323

AIRMAN

Sir, that your law is good we well believe;
But how to keep it? Will the seed of Cain
Forgive, or seek forgiveness, or be meek?
Was it worth while – forgive my bluntness, sir –
That God should be made man, only to say
To man, 'Be perfect', when it can't be done?
A rough-and-ready rule that can be kept
Is something; but impossible demands
Will only serve to make us desperate.

PERSONA

Only Myself can keep My law in you;
Merely to hear My words and nod approval
Is nothing – 'tis a house that's built on sand.
I must be closer to you than your marrow,
The sight of your eyes, the thought within your brain.
I say, unless you eat My flesh and blood
And make My substance and My self your own,
You cannot live. I am your bread, your wine;
I give my body to be broken for you
That I, in you, may break and give yourselves
For all the world. No man has greater love
Than he who lays his life down for his friends.

JV p.329

Carrying the Cross

Bind on the back of God the sins of the City;
Bind Him for Judas, bind Him for Herod, bind Him
For Caiaphas, Pilate and Cain; bind the wrong,
Bind the wrath and the tyranny, bind the treason,
Bind the fear and the folly, the greed and the grudging,
The diseases and the death, the lies told in the market,
The familiar fireside slander, the traffic in blood,
The lazing, the lust, the cruel insatiate wheels,
The needs and neglects, the callousness of the possessors,
The envy of dispossession; bind the City,
The plundered earth, the dull disconsolate streets,
The splitting wood and the sweating stone, the smoke
And the reek, the glare and the glitter, the filth of the kennels,
The slums and the stews, the soil and shame of the City.

Bind on the back of God the laws of the City;
Bind Him for the priest; bind Him for the assessor,
For the upright judge and the incorruptible jury;
Bind Him in fetters, bind Him in just retribution,
Bind Him in discipline; bind the surgeon's knife,
The physic, the fasting; bind the holy war,
The weapons of defence, the armies of occupation;
Bind Him in power and in penalty; bind the rod,
The rule and the righteous judgment; bind the City,
The school, the asylum, the spires of the Cathedral,
The Courts of Justice, the police, the prison, the dock,
The gallows, the stern and salutary institutions,
The state and the standards, the shambles and sewers of the City.

JV pp. 341–2

The Airman's death

This is it. This is what we have always feared—
The moment of surrender, the helpless moment
When there is nothing to do but to let go. . . .
'Into Thy hands' – into another's hand
No matter whose; the enemy's hand, death's hand,
God's. . . . The one moment not to be evaded
Which says, 'You must,' the moment not of choice
When we must choose to do the thing we must
And will to let our own will go. Let go.
It is no use now clinging to the controls,
Let some one else take over. Take, then, take . . .
There, that is done . . . into Thy hand, O God.

JV p. 348

. . . speak! speak peace, O Lord, to the City

I the Image of the Godhead bodily
In whom the Godhead and the Manhood are one,
Born into time, begotten from everlasting
Of the Father's love, by the gift of the Holy Ghost,
In whom all Heaven subsists; who, being in Heaven,
And being made Man, descending out of Heaven,
Bore for man's sake to set My feet in Hell:
I the end, and I the beginning of all things,
Call My Christendom out of the waste places,
Call the dry bones back from Jehoshaphat,
Call My multitudes in the valley of decision,
Call you home to Myself, in whom your selves
Find their true selfhood and their whole desire.
What has astonished you? Shall not I keep faith
Now with My chosen, and give you all you chose
When you laid your will in Mine in the moment of choice
And bade Me choose for you? When you chose Me
You were made Mine; and I am yours for ever.
That which you gave, you have. All you who choose
To bear with me the bitter burden of things
In patience, or, being burdened without choice,
Choose only to be patient, whether you give
Your bodies to be burned, your hearts to be broken,
Or only stand and wait in the market-place
For work or bread in a long tediousness,
Think, it is I that stand and suffer with you,
Adding My innocence to redeem your guilt,
And yours with Mine, to ransom all mankind.
This is My courtesy, to make you partners
With God in your own rescue, nor do anything
But by your love and by your will consenting.
Come then, and take again your own sweet will
That once was buried in the spicy grave
With Me, and now is risen with me, more sweet
Than myrrh and cassia; come, receive again
All your desires, but better than your dreams,
All your lost loves, but lovelier than you knew,

All your fond hopes, but higher than your hearts
Could dare to frame them; all your City of God
Built by your faith but nobler than you planned.
Instead of your justice, you shall have charity;
Instead of your happiness you shall have joy;
Instead of your peace the emulous exchange
Of love; and I will give you the morning star.
Rise up, My mother Mary and come away,
Rise up, My daughter Eve and My sweet son Adam,
Rise up, My city, rise up, My church, My bride!
For the time of your singing is come, and My bright angels
Unwinter hosanna in the perpetual spring;
So enter My Father's house, and there take seizure
Of the crown laid up and the incorruptible treasure,
Where the endless Now is one with the moment's measure,
The truth with the image, the City one with the King.

JV pp. 349–51

CHOIR
Well done, good and faithful servants,
Enter now into the joy of your Lord.

The earth is yours, and the voice of sounding metal,
The gold and the iron and the brass, the clarions of conquest.
You shall command the eagles, you shall laugh at leviathan;
The striped tiger shall sit with velvet feet
At the hearth; you shall be made glad with the grape and the
   wheat;
Nothing at all shall offend you, no snare shall enmesh –
You shall praise God with the glorious and holy flesh.

The sea is yours and the waters, with the voice
Of the dropping rain; O lute and harp, awake!
Rivers shall not drown love, nor the floods o'erwhelm it;
You shall be poured out with the cataract, ride the tide,
Run with the stream; beauty shall mould and hold you;
You shall fill up the cup of all delight; your art
Shall praise God with the moving and sensitive heart.

The air is yours, the wind that bends the cedars
And breathes in the reeds, the bodiless mighty voice
That comes and goes unseen; you shall be keen
To pierce and pass between a thought and a thought;
Nothing shall stay you or stain; by south and north,
East, west, you shall go forth and turn again –
You shall praise God with the searching and subtle brain.

The fire is yours; the fire mounts up to God
Beyond the angels of the spheres, whose strings
Are tuned too deep and high for mortal ears;
You shall possess that music; you shall go
Secure among the mysteries; the sun
Shall harm you not by day nor the moon by night –
Your soul shall praise God, and your spirit shall fathom the depth
   and the height.

JV pp. 351–2

159

Apart from the exposition of the doctrine of the Atonement in *The Just Vengeance* there are two passages out of those just quoted which relate especially to Dante's *Divine Comedy*. The first of these comes at the point of acceptance of the plea of the Chorus by Mary, when this is acknowledged by the Choir's singing of the first few lines of St Bernard's Hymn to the Blessed Virgin from Canto 33 of *Paradise*. The first twenty-one lines of the Hymn Dorothy Sayers was to translate and publish privately as a Christmas card in 1949, and Barbara Reynolds was therefore able to insert them into her translation of *Paradise*. It is included here in the selections from Dante's work (see p. 175). Just as Dorothy Sayers believed that *this* man was very God, so she believed in 'the personal operation of the Mother of God' (Pg Introduction, p. 39). Mary was the supreme but not the only symbol of grace for Dante, for amongst those human persons who mediate grace to him (H 2, Commentaries, p. 82) there are especially in the *Comedy* Beatrice, his particular God-bearing image, and Lucy, illuminating grace, who together with Mary are 'a threefold image of Divine Grace in its various manifestations'. They even formed an analogy of the Trinity as Theotokos/mother of God; derived God-bearer; and bond and messenger between the two.

The second passage to note in *The Just Vengeance* is the concluding song of the choir, on the capacity to praise God with 'the glorious and holy flesh', 'the moving and sensitive heart', and 'the searching and subtle brain'. This passage is her response to Canto 14 of *Paradise*, part of which is also included here (see pp. 171–2). Dante had provoked her to this statement of sacramental theology in a way which excels her earlier paraphrases of the creed. Dorothy Sayers suffered from no illusions about her own life and the life of others, or about the extent to which some of our ills are likely to be self-inflicted, or inflicted on others. She believed, however, that pain and tears do not have the last word, and Dante's Solomon enabled her to express this conviction. In Canto 14 he is simply the one who has a voice 'Mild as the Angel's was, belike, to Mary', but he has been identified in Canto 10 by St Thomas Aquinas, no less (P 10. 109–14):

160

The fifth light yonder, brightest of us all,
   So breathes our love that every man on ground
   Thirsts for his news: that mind majestical

There dwells, in whom such wisdom did abound,
   None ever rose in any generation,
   If the truth speak true, to insight so profound.

Dorothy Sayers' notes inform us of discussion among theologians as to whether Solomon was saved or damned, whether he had repented of idolatry and his other sins. Perplexity about the presence and interpretation of the Song of Songs in the canon of scripture was a complicating factor for some, but not for Dante. The biblical text to reread here is 1 Kings 3:5–13 where God asks what Solomon wants as king. Wisely he asks not for long life for himself, nor riches, nor the life of his enemies, but for understanding in judgement. God replies that he has given him 'a wise and understanding heart; so that there was none like thee before thee, neither after thee shall any arise like unto thee'. Royal and divinely given wisdom in his person amongst the blessed is able 'to solve Dante's doubt as to the splendour of the body after the resurrection' (P 14, Commentaries, p. 182).

It is important to keep *Paradise* in focus in reading *The Divine Comedy* because, as Dorothy Sayers unequivocally insists, the grim substructure of hell, the equivalent of a few days spent among the cellars and sewers of a city (sordidness, suffocation, rats, fetor and gloom) is only there 'for the sake of the city whose walls and spires stand up and take the morning'. Even the saints in paradise are preoccupied with politics in church and state, and the 'city' is the 'place' where they experience the vision of God (H Introduction p. 11). That apart, there are a number of themes in Dante which we can identify as being of special importance to her. Dante recalls us to the point that our choices can be decisive to all eternity and that damnation is to be recognized as a terrible possibility for and within oneself. Marks of Hell are the denial and refusal of God incarnate – Christ seen not as Redeemer but as the 'Enemy Power'; the final refusal and thus incapacity for the central act of worship, the bodily receiving of God's substance in the sacrament of bread and wine; and the appalling horrors of 'enfleshment' (as distinct from resurrection) so hideously represented in the Cantos of *Hell*. God risks that assent to the reality that one is a created being, whose end is to mirror God's glory, will be refused, or given with a bad grace, plunging the soul into frustration and misery. The final alternative to the vision of God is, as she paraphrased Boethius, 'the perfect and simultaneous possession of one's own will for ever' (IPD p. 67). However baffling the final refusal of God remains, she found in Dante the imagination and the poetic skill to represent it, in his circles of perverse and petrified choice, narrowing down to Hell's frozen centre. At the very bottom is the corruption of beauty itself, aping the glory of the Trinity, a monstrous three-headed parody fixed in his inimitable self-will, champing the traitors in his jaws: 'the six wings of his immortal seraphhood beat savagely, powerless to lift him out of the ice of his obduracy, and increasing that ice by the wind of their beating', idiot and slobbering horror (PSS pp. 239–40):

Satan

The Emperor of the sorrowful realm was there,
  Out of the girding ice he stood breast-high,
  And to his arm alone the giants were

Less comparable than to a giant I;
  Judge then how huge the stature of the whole
  That to so huge a part bears symmetry.

If he was once as fair as now he's foul,
  And dared outface his Maker in rebellion,
  Well may he be the fount of all our dole.

And marvel 'twas, out-marvelling a million,
  When I beheld three faces in his head;
  The one in front was scarlet like vermilion;

And two, mid-centred on the shoulders, made
  Union with this, and each with either fellow
  Knit at the crest, in triune junction wed.

The right was of a hue 'twixt white and yellow;
  The left was coloured like the men who dwell
  Where Nile runs down from source to sandy shallow.

From under each sprang two great wings that well
  Befitted such a monstrous bird as that;
  I ne'er saw ship with such a spread of sail.

Plumeless and like the pinions of a bat
  Their fashion was; and as they flapped and whipped
  Three winds went rushing over the icy flat

And froze up all Cocytus; and he wept
  From his six eyes, and down his triple chin
  Runnels of tears and bloody slaver dripped.

H 34. 28–54

Dorothy Sayers could not claim that the doctrine of Purgatory was taught by Christ with the same robustness as she could make the claim about Hell, given the seriousness of Christ's judgement on sin in the Gospels. Her case for Purgatory rested on grounds of practical charity, and 'our sense of the communion between the blessed dead and ourselves' (see IPD pp. 75–76). The charity of prayer enables the souls in Purgatory to perform their penance better. Although Dante's Purgatory is a place of great beauty in which music can begin after the hell of hideous, chaotic and incessant noise from which he has emerged, the pains of Purgatory are like those of Hell, and little lighter in some cases. The difference is in the attitude of those who suffer these pains (like Faustus earlier), who want their crippling illusions to be burned away, so that judgement and will may be free, and the soul 'may endure unscathed the unveiled light of reality' (Pg Introduction, p. 16). Given the examples of pride (Faustus, William, Judas) we have already seen, it is particularly appropriate both to read Dante's paraphrase of the Lord's Prayer in Canto 11 and to connect it with Dante's own love for Beatrice, and the effect this had on him. The proud have to accept humility as a gift above all, having learned with great difficulty that

> just beneath the crust of our civilisation the fires of Hell burn to an unimaginable depth, and that for the fruition of joy it is not sufficient to exort men to be temperate and reasonable. To know the good is not necessarily to do it . . . nor even, perhaps, effectively to desire it. Our virtues stultify themselves, and 'the evil that we would not, that we do'.

> 'Dante's Virgil', FPD p. 61

The prayer of the Proud

'Our Father, dwelling in the Heavens, nowise
  As circumscribed, but as the things above,
  Thy first effects, are dearest in Thine eyes,

Hallowed Thy name be and the Power thereof,
  By every creature, as right meet it is
  We praise the tender effluence of Thy Love.

Let come to us, let come Thy Kingdom's peace;
  If it come not, we've no power of our own
  To come to it, for all our subtleties.

Like as with glad Hosannas at Thy throne
  Thine angels offer up their wills alway,
  So let men offer theirs, that Thine be done.

Our daily manna give to us this day,
  Without which he that through this desert wild
  Toils most to speed goes backward on his way.

As we, with all our debtors reconciled,
  Forgive, do Thou forgive us, nor regard
  Our merits, but upon our sins look mild.

Put not our strength, too easily ensnared
  And overcome, to proof with the old foe;
  But save us from him, for he tries it hard.

This last prayer is not made for us – know,
  Dear Lord, that it is needless – but for those
  Who still remain behind us we pray so.'

                                    Pg 11. 1–24

165

Dorothy Sayers reminds us of the effect of Beatrice's *salute* (both 'salutation' *and* 'salvation' is meant) upon Dante, even the hope of it. In his own words:

> I say that when she appeared from any direction, then, in the hope of her wondrous salutation, there was no enemy left to me; rather there smote into me a flame of charity, which made me forgive every person who had ever injured me; and if at that moment anybody had put a question to me about anything whatsoever, my answer would have been simply 'Love', with a countenance clothed in humility.

H Introduction, p. 28, quoting from the *Vita Nuova* XI

So when Dorothy Sayers comments on the point in Canto 12 where the Angel of Humility erases the sign of pride from off Dante's forehead, she says we need to recall the contexts, such as the one above, in which Dante uses the word 'humility' to understand the 'shimmering radiance of its angel' and the connotations of the word with peace, sweetness, and 'a kind of suspension of the heart in a delightful tranquility' (Pg 12, Commentaries). Meekness within, and charity to those without are signs of grace, with the soul able to adore and love a fellow-creature whose bodily presence is somehow felt to be a vehicle of grace (PSS p. 49–50).

Dante's relationship with Beatrice is a complicated and fascinating subject in its own right, since as Charles Williams has remarked of the poet who was a grown man with a wife (Gemma) and four children of his own, there was probably more of Gemma in Beatrice than Dante himself quite knew (Pg Introduction, p. 35). Dante's love for Beatrice had to be that of a man who had loved a child when he was himself a child, had seen her married to another man, and then endured her death as a young woman. A gesture as simple as a kiss may be both the image of a sin – say, the indulgent dallying with temptation of Paolo and Francesca (Canto 5 of *Hell*) or the image of salvation, as in Canto 26 of *Purgatory*:

166

> I see each shade, on swiftness all intent,
>> Kiss one from out the other troop, and go,
>> Not pausing, with this brief salute content.

Pg 26. 31–3

The meaning of Beatrice's salutation for him he could see in the exchange of a kiss between other human beings as grace-bearers for one another, or as in the case of Francesca and her lover, the source of one another's damnation rather than salvation.

We have noted in connection with *The Just Vengeance* that it is Beatrice who explains the doctrine of the Atonement to Dante, and in 1944 Dorothy Sayers wrote a particularly entertaining letter in which we can recapture her pleasure in Dante's Beatrice:

> I had an alarming vision just now in my bath. I had *both* Dante and Milton as evacuees. After a long wet day, which they had whiled away by reading each other's works, they sat one on either side of the fire, Dante like a mournful eagle in captivity, and Milton like a bull in the arena, whose eyes were beginning to roll dangerously. I said nervously, 'Well, well, it's been wretched weather, hasn't it?' Whereat Milton, ignoring me, suddenly opened his mouth and told Dante exactly what he thought of young women who gave their boy-friends lectures in theology. When he had finished, Dante rose to his feet, slowly unfolding to his full height, until, like a black pillar, his form obscured the light of the fire, and then he spoke – but, like the *grido* of the sphere of Jupiter, the sound was so terrible that the sense escaped me.

Reynolds, p. 186

Given those earlier essays, 'Are Women Human?' and 'The Human-not-quite-human' she was delighted to find in Dante a man who could differ from Aquinas in his evaluation of women (FPD p. 38). Of the biology reflected in Canto 25 of *Purgatory* (the theory that the female's part in generation was purely passive) she merely noted that popular psychology and popular moral standards still remained faithful to this

167

scientific theory, presumably meaning the association of the female/feminine with receiving and the male/masculine with giving. She need only note it and not discuss it, because it has nothing to do with the Dante's understanding of the way in which Beatrice represented for him the integrity of the intellectual, emotional, bodily and sacramental. She cleverly compares Beatrice to Elizabeth Bennet in *Pride and Prejudice* – 'Had you behaved in a more gentlemanlike manner . . .'; and, 'She remembered that he had yet to learn to be laughed at' (Pg Introduction, p. 34). These accents are noticeable in Beatrice's first and regal words to Dante in Canto 30 of *Purgatory*: 'Look on us well; we are indeed, we are Beatrice', which precipitate Dante's tears, as well they might. Nonetheless, nothing inhibits Dante's ability to recognize not only her intellectual competence, but also her sacramental character, female and feminine though she indeed is. She is at once the Florentine woman he loved; the one who was for him (as he in turn could be for someone else) the God-bearing image who reveals the divine in God's creation; and the one who signified the sacrament of the altar. For Dante, her loss in death seems to have been the lived experience of the denial of the images which after progress in the 'negative way' can then be re-affirmed in the search for the vision of God. It would be very important for Dorothy Sayers to identify the point at which Dante reflects on the Eucharist, and it is in the Pageant of the Sacrament of Canto 30 of *Purgatory*:

Beatrice is the particular type and image of that whole sacramental principle of which the Host itself is the greater Image. The Eucharist is displayed nowhere else in the poem because it is displayed here. In the literal sense, what Dante looks upon is Beatrice; but on the three allegorical levels at which (Dante says) the poem is to be interpreted, she is Sacrament. Morally (i.e. as regards the way of the individual soul) she is, to Dante and to each one of us, the manifestation of the Divine glory in whatsoever beloved thing becomes to every man his own particular sacramental experience. Historically (i.e. in the world of human society) she is the Sacrament of the Altar. And those who say that in this passage Beatrice represents the Church are not wrong; for I think

168

that Dante is here reflecting that older, Apostolic conception of the Eucharist, still surviving in Aquinas, which looks upon it, not exclusively as the commemoration of a single act in time, but as the presentation in Christ to God of Christ's true Body the Church (the *verum corpus*), which is made in the offertory of the bread and wine, so that, as St Augustine says: 'being joined to His Body and made His members, we may *be* what we *receive*'. Thirdly, on the mystical level, Beatrice is here the whole doctrine of the Way of Affirmation – the union of the soul with God in and through all the images.

'Dante and Charles Williams', FPD pp. 192–3

In explanation of the Way of Affirmation she cited three great Christian doctrines, the first being the doctrine of a true creation, made by God, as an artist makes a work of art, and given independent existence. Every creature possesses a self which however much 'in-godded' in Dante's phrase, is never lost in God, and so can image God to one degree or another (FPD p. 187). The third image is the doctrine of the Trinity, which 'affirms that the Image actually exists within the very mystery of the Godhead Itself', and in the spheres of the Trinity of Canto 33 of *Paradise* Dante found a focus for his gaze 'limned with our image', his soul confronted with the immediate presence of God. To preface the words of Solomon on the resurrection, however, her words about the second doctrine, that of Incarnation, are most suitable:

The second doctrine is that of the Incarnation, whereby God Himself became manifest in mortal flesh. In that flesh his glory dwelt, and was seen so dwelling by Peter and James and John at the Transfiguration, when their eyes were opened to behold it. It was always there – it was not really He that was changed, but their sight. From the Incarnation springs the whole doctrine of sacraments – the indwelling of the mortal by the immortal, of the material by the spiritual, the phenomenal by the real. After an analogous manner, we all bear about with us not only the immortal soul but also the glorified body in which we shall be known at the Resurrection, though now it is known only, to God, or to those to whom love may reveal it. It is this that lies at the bottom of Dante's whole Beatrician Vision: because he loved the mortal Florentine girl, it was given to him to behold her, as it were, walking the earth in her body of glory. And this is why, in the *Commedia*, a stress so disconcerting to the minds of those who like their religion to be very 'spiritual' is laid continually upon her bodily beauty. A sure mark of Catholic Christianity is the honouring of the 'holy and glorious flesh', and indeed of all material things, because they are sacraments and symbols of the Divine glory.

'Dante and Charles Williams', FPD p. 187

Solomon on the resurrection

As carol-dancers in their merry ploy
   Break into music, and so wind and wheel
   With livelier gestures, through access of joy,

So, at that prompt and worshipful appeal
   New pleasure did the circling hallows show,
   In wondrous song exprest and swifter reel.

He that laments because we die below
   To live up yonder, sees not how they spring,
   Those showers eternal, freshening where they flow.

The One and Two and Three that there is King,
   And lives for ever Three and Two and One,
   By naught contained, containing everything,

Was three times hymned in such melodious tone
   By every spirit there, as well might carry
   Praise of a worth past all comparison.

And then, from the divinest luminary
   Of the inner ring, I heard a voice arise
   Mild as the Angel's was, belike, to Mary:

'Long as shall last the feast of Paradise,
   Even so long,' it said, 'our love shall lace
   This radiance round us for our festal guise.

Its brightness with our fervour shall keep pace,
   Fervour with sight, sight so enlarge the mesh
   Of its own worth as it hath more of grace;

And when we put completeness on afresh,
   All the more gracious shall our person be,
   Reclothed in the holy and glorious flesh;

Whereby shall grow the unearned gift and free
   The Highest Good bestows – that gift of light
   By which we are enabled Him to see;

Hence must we ever win to more of sight,
   And by more sight more fervour still acquire,
   And by more fervour radiance still more bright.

But, as the living coal which shoots forth fire
   Outgoes it in candescence, and is found
   Whole at the heart of it with shape entire,

The lustre which already swathes us round
   Shall be outlustred by the flesh, which long
   Day after day now moulders underground;

Nor shall that light have power to do us wrong,
   Since for all joys that shall delight us then
   The body's organs will be rendered strong.

P 14. 19–58

Dorothy Sayers wrote of Dante's achievement that 'Excitement about *getting* to Heaven is not rare in works of literature: excitement about *being* in Heaven is a much rarer thing' (FPD p. 31). At the end of the day Dante, like the Jesus who has the conversation with Lazarus in *The Man Born to be King* (p. 108), finds joy at the heart of reality, laughter, inebriation, 'this riot of charity and hilarity', a fountain of happiness bursting and bubbling:

> With Dante it is for once not true that to travel hopefully is better than to arrive. We arrive, and the arrival is satisfactory. The adventure of the passionate intellect is achieved, and it is so because Dante's passions really are seated in this intellect, and not, as with so many of us, marooned in his heart and liver, without means of access to the brain. On whatever rarified flights the story-teller sets out, he can take his whole equipment with him.
>
> '. . . and telling you a story', FPD p. 35

So after St Bernard's prayer to the Virgin, we conclude with her poem for Timothy-cat, related to some lines from Canto 28 of *Paradise*:

> The dances which remain display to view
> Princedoms, Archangels, and one circle more
> With Angels' jubilation is filled through.
>
> And all these orders upwards gaze with awe,
> As downwards each prevails upon the rest,
> Whence all are drawn to God and to Him draw.
>
> P 28. 124–9

All look upon God in the measure of the knowledge and love which they have by the grace given to them and their own good will; all are drawn up with the cords of love by those above them, and themselves draw those below them. The Heavens draw Man; and Man was made 'lord of creation' that he might draw up the whole material creation. What Man in his fallen nature cannot

173

do of himself, Christ does in man, until the resurrection of the 'holy and glorious flesh' and the 'reconciliation of all things' to God in Christ, in a new Heaven and a new earth.

'The Meaning of Heaven and Hell', IPD pp. 59–60

In an essay on Dante and Charles Williams, who had inspired her reading of Dante, she reflected on the hierarchy of Dante's theology, and that the communication of glory is from above downwards (FPD p. 194). Williams had glimpsed a vision of humanity in which the relationship of higher to lower is fluid, as it would surely need to be for the mutuality of prayer expressed in the 'I in-thee me as thou in-meëst thee' of Canto 9 of *Paradise*. Not only could we say that God desires that love should flow upon all our fellow-creatures (including a domestic pet as an example) but more pointedly, that human beings especially need to acknowledge the ways in which in love they may generously exchange places with one another on the ladder of ascent. If Dorothy Sayers is right in reading Dante as meaning that the images and means of salvation may be recognized, as he did, in both women and men, then we need not suppose that a great text of the past has nothing to offer to a living and vital religious tradition of today, and the attempt we might make to attend to God in a world we may misconstrue as bereft of signs of divine presence.

St Bernard's prayer to the Virgin

'O Virgin Mother, Daughter of thy Son,
   Lowliest and loftiest of created stature,
   Fixed goal to which the eternal counsels run,

Thou art that She by whom our human nature
   Was so ennobled that it might become
   The Creator to create himself his creature.

Thy sides were made a shelter to relume
   The Love whose warmth within the timeless peace
   Quickened the seed of this immortal bloom;

High noon of charity to those in bliss,
   And upon earth, to men in mortal plight,
   A living spring of hope, thy presence is.

Lady, so great thou art and such thy might,
   The seeker after grace who shuns thy knee
   May aim his prayer, but fails to wing the flight.

Not only does thy succour flow out free
   To him who asks, but many a time the aid
   Fore-runs the prayer, such largesse is in thee.

All ruth, all mercy are in thee displayed,
   And all munificence; in thee is knit
   Together all that's good in all that's made.'

P 33. 1–21

For Timothy, in the Coinherence

Tutti tirati sono, e tutti tirano.
Paradiso, XXVIII, 129

Consider, O Lord, Timothy, Thy servants' servant.
  (We give him this title, as to Thy servant the Pope,
  Not knowing a better. Him too Thy ministers were observant
To vest in white and adorn with a silk cope.)

Thy servant lived with Thy servants in the exchange
  Of affection; he condescended to them from the dignity
  Of an innocent mind; they bent to him with benignity
From the rarefied Alps of their intellectual range.

Hierarchy flourished, with no resentment
  For the unsheathed claw or the hand raised in correction,
  Small wild charities took root beneath the Protection,
Garden-escapes from the Eden of our contentment.

Daily we came short in the harder human relation,
  Only in this easier obeying, Lord, Thy commands;
  Meekly we washed his feet, meekly he licked our hands –
Beseech Thee, overlook not this mutual grace of salvation.

Canst Thou accept our pitiful good behaving,
  Stooping to share at our hand that best we keep for the beast?
  Sir, receive the alms, though least, and bestowed on the least;
Save us, and save somehow with us the means of our saving.

Dante in the Ninth Heaven beheld love's law
  Run up and down on the infinite golden stairway;
  Angels, men, brutes, plants, matter, up that fairway
All by love's cords are drawn, said he, and draw.

Thou that before the Fall didst make pre-emption
  Of Adam, restore the privilege of the Garden,
  Where he to the beasts was namer, tamer and warden;
Buy back his household and all in the world's redemption.

When the Ark of the new life grounds upon Ararat
  Grant us to carry into the rainbow's light,
  In a basket of gratitude, the small, milk-white
Silken identity of Timothy, our cat.

The Listener 15 March 1973

EPILOGUE

=

In this anthology we have seen something of Dorothy Sayers'
work as a writer of theology, of her development from her
early Oxford days through to her own brilliant appropriation
of Dante, and her skill in communicating her own enlarged
theological vision after reading him. No greater tribute could
be paid to her than that we ourselves turn again to the whole
range of that last phase of her work, and read it thoroughly
for ourselves – especially her 'introductory' and 'further'
papers on Dante, which we have met in short extracts.

To conclude, however, is a complete essay which is free of
the complexities of those essays in their entirety, but which
turns us full circle to the beginning of her career. The opening
extracts in this anthology were a 'Hymn in Contemplation
of Sudden Death' and a poem about the salvation of 'Judas'.
Dante's Judas, together with other traitors, was champed in
Satan's jaws, and we can imagine that reading Dante and
reflecting on the events of her own lifetime, which included
two world wars, perhaps re-focussed Sayers' sense not only
of the ecstasy of heaven but of the possibility of damnation.
She has an excellent essay on 'The Meaning of Heaven and
Hell' in her introductory papers on Dante, but our concluding essay on 'Christian Belief about Heaven and Hell' was
published for a wide non-specialist audience in 1957, the year
of her own death. We may suppose that it distils what she
had learned and relearned from him on these awesome topics
as part of her life-long exploration of Christianity as a
religion for adult minds.

Christian Belief About Heaven and Hell

If we are to understand the Christian doctrine about what happens at death, we must first rid our minds of every concept of time and space as we know them. Our time and space have no independent reality: they belong to the universe and were created with it. Take down any novel you like from the shelf. The story it tells may cover the events of a few hours or of many years; it may range over a few acres or the whole globe. But all that space-time is contained within the covers of the book, and has no contact at any point with the space-time in which you are living. It, and the whole universe of action which goes on inside the book, are made things, deriving their existence from the mind of their maker.

Christians believe that our universe of space and time is, similarly, a made thing. It is quite 'real' so far as it goes, but its reality is dependent on that of its Maker, who is alone real in His own right. They also believe that the soul of Man has been so made that it is capable of entering into the true Reality which we call 'Heaven' or 'the presence of God'. So that when we die, it is not as though the characters and action of the book were 'continued in our next' like a serial; it is as though they came out from the book to partake of the real existence of their author.

If this real existence involves anything at all corresponding to 'time' and 'space', these do not coincide with ours in any way, and we can have no conception of them. We call them 'eternity' and 'infinity' simply to mark their total unlikeness to anything that we experience; and when we speak of God's 'time' as an 'eternal present' we mean to exclude every idea of duration in *our* time.

*   *   *

All this was understood and insisted on by instructed Christians up to the end of the Middle Ages (e.g. by Boethius in the sixth century and Dante in the fourteenth). It was only after the Reformation and the Renaissance of Learning that childishly literal notions of a localised Heaven extended in measurable time began to creep out of popular mythology into the minds of educated people.

Accordingly, Christians do not very much care for the term 'survival', which suggests a continuation along the old lines of space and time. It is less misleading to speak of coming out of time into eternity. Heaven is the abiding contemplation of, and union with, that total perfection which we call 'God', who is the unconditioned Reality containing and upholding the conditioned realities of the space-time universe which He made.

It is in this sense that we speak of Christianity as an 'other-worldly' religion – not because it denies the significance and importance of the created universe, but because it places the centre of reality not within that universe, but in God. Our senses, assisted by the sciences, teach us to follow 'the story' from inside, and to see it as an orderly sequence of events; and as such it will appear to be a self-contained network of cause and effect. But the *real* cause of those events – the intention in the mind of the author – can only be very dimly inferred from the data within the story, unless the author should choose to reveal himself by becoming a character within his own creation; and this, of course, Christians believe that our Maker has done.

But in this life, as T. S. Eliot has said, 'Human kind cannot bear very much reality. We have to be trained to encounter it.' It is not merely that, being finite, we cannot apprehend reality, but that, being sinful, we are unwilling to accept it. For, to accept reality, it is necessary to acknowledge that the source and centre of our being is not in ourselves, but in God. Sin is the self-sufficiency which urges us to reject this idea and to delude ourselves with the flattering fantasy that Man's being is centred in himself – that he can be 'as God'. Thus our outlook is not only finite, but violently distorted, and evils are called into existence – evils which, though from the point of view of eternal reality they are seen to be lies and illusions, yet within the created frame of things are, unhappily, quite as real as anything else in the material universe.

Our 'training' to encounter reality is thus made much more difficult by our insistence on clinging to a false idea of the self. We have not only everything to learn, but also much to unlearn. The will and judgment need to be purged as well as strengthened before we can become possessed of our true selves and endure to enter the heavenly presence of God, where we shall 'know even as we are known'. This training is the work of time, and its aim is the freeing of the will and judgment from those errors and perversions which render it incapable of facing the Divine Reality.

If the training is not completed at the time of death, it will have to be completed after death; that is why any attempt to hold the

180

spirits 'earthbound' – by 'calling them up' at séances, or even by importunate and possessive grief – is to do them wrong by delaying their entry into beatitude. But sooner or later, if beatitude is what we truly want, we shall get it; for it is what God wants for us and, as St Paul says, no created thing, whether of time, space or spirit, can separate us from His love.

But do we truly want it? At bottom – yes, we do, for it is the end for which we were made and without which we cannot be happy or complete. 'In every soul that shall be saved,' said the Lady Julian of Norwich, 'there is a godly will that never assented to sin, nor ever shall,' and it is this will which has to be set free so that it may become united to God.

*   *   *

There remains, however, the terrible possibility that the continual indulgence of the false self may so weaken the true God-ward will that it becomes impotent, so that, in the moment of death which is the moment of final choice, the soul will shrink away from the presence of God and refuse beatitude. If so, we shall have what we have willed to have. We shall have to live for ever with the sinful self that we have chosen; and this is called Hell.

God *sends* nobody to Hell; only a wicked ignorance can suggest that He would do to us the very thing He died to save us from. But He has so made us that what in the end we choose, that in the end we shall have. If we enter the state called Hell, it is because we have willed to do so.

Neither can He force any soul into beatitude against its will; for He has nothing but Himself to give it, and it is precisely the light of His presence which the self-centred soul can know only as burning and judgment. So the Lady Julian said that in her visions she 'saw no Hell but Sin,' and St Catherine of Genoa said that the fire of the torment was the light of God as experienced by those who reject it.

*   *   *

Christians believe that 'in the end of the world' God will make 'a new heaven and a new earth', and that the body will then be raised from the dead and be united to the soul, so that the whole man will be restored in his completeness. About this we know very little. The only resurrection-body of which we have any knowledge is that of the risen Christ, and it is clear from the Gospel narrative that, although it could manifest itself in our time and space, its relation to them was of a very special kind, and that it did not belong to our universe at all. St Paul calls the resurrection body 'a spiritual body', and stresses its *difference*: 'It is sown in corruption, it is raised in incorruption: it is sown in weakness, it is raised in power.'

In any case, we need not puzzle our wits to find a time and place for it within the universe, because, in the end of time, that universe 'shall be rolled together as a scroll' (that is, as a reader shuts up a volume when he has finished with it), and God will write a new book.

The Great Mystery of Life Hereafter, pp. 11–18

BIBLIOGRAPHY AND ACKNOWLEDGEMENTS

=

The following, in chronological order, are the works by or about Dorothy Sayers that are quoted or cited in this book. An abridgement given after a title is that which is used in the present book. Page references, where given, refer to the first edition, except that the four plays marked here FSP are cited from *Four Sacred Plays* (Gollancz 1948). Quotations from the translation of Dante's *Divine Comedy* have the Canto number followed by the verse numbers. Publication rights in all the writings of Dorothy L. Sayers are held by David Higham Associates Ltd. Permission to reproduce the passages used in this collection is acknowledged with thanks.

Op. I, B.H. Blackwell, 1916

The Nine Tailors, (NT), Victor Gollancz, 1934

Gaudy Night (GN), Victor Gollancz, 1935

The Zeal of Thy House (ZH), Victor Gollancz, 1938 (FSP 1948)

'The Dogma is the Drama' (1938), quoted from *Creed or Chaos? and other Essays in Popular Theology* (CC), Methuen, 1947

'The Greatest Drama Ever Staged', Hodder and Stoughton, 1938, reprinted in *Creed or Chaos?* (as above)

'The Triumph of Easter', Hodder and Stoughton, 1938, reprinted in *Creed or Chaos?* (as above)

'The Other Six Deadly Sins', reprinted in *Creed or Chaos?* (as above)

He That Should Come (HTSC), Victor Gollancz, 1939 (FSP 1948)

The Devil to Pay (DP), Victor Gollancz, 1939 (FSP 1948)

The Mind of the Maker (MM), Methuen, 1941

(Contribution in) *Malvern 1941: The Life of the Church and Order of Society* (ML), Longmans, Green & Co, 1941

'Lord, I thank Thee' in S. Jameson (ed): *London Calling*, Harper and Brothers, 1942

'Vocation in Work' in A. E. Baker (ed.), *A Christian Basis for the Post War World*, SCM Press, 1942

The Man Born to be King (MBK), Victor Gollancz, 1943

The Just Vengeance (JV), Victor Gollancz, 1946 (FSP 1948)

Unpopular Opinions (UO), Victor Gollancz, 1946

Dante: The Divine Comedy I : Hell (H), Penguin Books, 1949

The Emperor Constantine (EC), Victor Gollancz, 1951

Introduction to C. M. Duncan-Jones: *Richard of Chichester*, Faith Press, 1953

Introductory Papers on Dante (IPD), Methuen, 1954

Dante: The Divine Comedy II : Purgatory (Pg), Penguin Books, 1955

Further Papers on Dante (FPD), Methuen, 1957

'Christian Belief about Heaven and Hell' in *The Great Mystery of Life Hereafter*, Hodder & Stoughton 1957

Dante: The Divine Comedy : Paradise (P), Penguin Books, 1962 (with Barbara Reynolds)

The Poetry of Search and the Poetry of Statement (PSS), Victor Gollancz, 1963

'For Timothy, in the Coinherence', published in *The Listener* on 15 March 1973

Ralph E. Hone: *Dorothy L. Sayers: A Literary Biography* (Hone) Kent State University Press, Ohio 44242, 1979

James Brabazon: *Dorothy L. Sayers: A Biography of a Courageous Woman* (Brabazon), Victor Gollancz, 1981

Barbara Reynolds: *The Passionate Intellect: Dorothy L. Sayers' Encounter with Dante* (Reynolds), Kent State University Press, Ohio 44242, 1989